About the Mountaineers

THE MOUNTAINEERS, founded in 1906, is a nonprofit outdoor activity and conservation club, whose mission is "to explore, study, preserve, and enjoy the natural beauty of the outdoors . . . " Based in Seattle, Washington, the club is now the third-largest such organization in the United States, with 15,000 members and five branches throughout Washington State.

The Mountaineers sponsors both classes and year-round outdoor activities in the Pacific Northwest, which include hiking, mountain climbing, ski-touring, snowshoeing, bicycling, camping, kayaking and canoeing, nature study, sailing, and adventure travel. The club's conservation division supports environmental causes through educational activities, sponsoring legislation, and presenting informational programs. All club activities are led by skilled, experienced volunteers, who are dedicated to promoting safe and responsible enjoyment and preservation of the outdoors.

If you would like to participate in these organized outdoor activities or the club's programs, consider a membership in The Mountaineers. For information and an application, write or call The Mountaineers, Club Headquarters, 300 Third Avenue West, Seattle, Washington 98119; (206) 284-6310.

The Mountaineers Books, an active, nonprofit publishing program of the club, produces guidebooks, instructional texts, historical works, natural history guides, and works on environmental conservation. All books produced by The Mountaineers are aimed at fulfilling the club's mission.

Send or call for our catalog of more than 300 outdoor titles:

The Mountaineers Books
1001 SW Klickitat Way, Suite 201
Seattle, WA 98134
800-553-4453
mbooks@mountaineers.org
www.mountaineersbooks.org

WASHINGTON'S MOUNT RAINIER: A Centennial Celebration
Tim McNulty and Pat O'hara
Large-format photographic celebration of the 100th anniversary of Mount Rainier National Park. The official book of the Centennial.

50 HIKES IN MOUNT RAINIER NATIONAL PARK
Fourth Edition, *Ira Spring and Harvey Manning*
Complete, authoritative hiking guide to the Northwest's most popular national park, with full-color photos and maps throughout.

100 CLASSIC HIKES IN WASHINGTON: North Cascades, Olympics, Mount Rainier & South Cascades, Alpine Lakes, Glacier Peak, *Ira Spring and Harvey Manning*
Spring and Manning present their favorite trails in this compendium of classic hikes. With full-color photos throughout.

Mount Rainier: A Climbing Guide, *Mike Gauthier*
Details 30 routes, with an emphasis on safety and minimum-impact climbing, by the lead climbing ranger at Mount Rainier National Park.

North Cascades Highway: Washington's Popular and Scenic Pass, *JoAnn Roe*
A comprehensive, regional history of the people, nature, and environment along the North Cascades Highway.

Field Guide to the Cascades & Olympics
Stephen Whitney
Describes and beautifully illustrates over 600 species of plants and animals found in mountains from Northern California to Southwest British Columbia.

Northwest Trees, *Stephen Arno and Ramona Hammerly*
Superb drawings enhance this study of the 35 conifers and broadleaves native to the Pacific Northwest.

Impressions of the North Cascades: Essays About a Northwest Landscape, *John Miles, Editor*
Essays by 13 contributors who interpret the North Cascades from the different perspectives of their disciplines and daily experiences.

A Year in
PARADISE

A Year in
PARADISE

by Floyd Schmoe

THE
MOUNTAINEERS

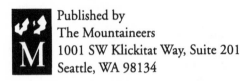
Published by
The Mountaineers
1001 SW Klickitat Way, Suite 201
Seattle, WA 98134

First cloth printing 1959 by Harper & Brothers
First paper printing 1968 by the Charles E. Tuttle Company, Inc.
Second paper printing 1979 by The Mountaineers, third printing 1999

Manufactured in Canada

Illustrations and maps by Floyd Schmoe
Book and cover design by Helen Cherullo
Book layout and cover production by Peggy Egerdahl

Cover photograph: Mt. Rainier and Paradise Meadow by Pat O'Hara

*Library of Congress Cataloging-in-Publication Data
on file at the Library of Congress*

Contents

List of Photographs

Foreword

FLOYD SCHMOE WORKED IN A VARIETY of positions within Mount Rainier National Park for many years. In 1919, when he first came to Mount Rainier, he was employed at Paradise as a caretaker, and later as a mountain guide by the Rainier National Park Company. He then returned to the University of Washington to obtain his forestry degree. His intense interest in Mount Rainier led him back to the park first as the District Ranger, and later as Mount Rainier's first Park Naturalist.

Writing out of his own experience and memories, Mr. Schmoe tells of the mountain as it is through the turning seasons—the long white frozen winters, the brief tumultuous springs, the equally brief summers glorious with blooms and invitations to adventure, the autumns with visitors gone and the life of the mountain restored to its ancient rhythm. Through this personal narrative runs comment on the many things which to him spell the charm of the region. The work is a reflection of Mr. Schmoe's personal philosophy for living in peace and wonderment of nature.

Today, visitors to Mount Rainier National Park will find the natural environment little changed though nearly 50 years have passed. Yet in this same 50 years our society has evolved at an ever quickening pace. As a newcomer to Mount Rainier I have found in this book a delightful introduction to a magnificent park.

More importantly, I have found a stimulus for reflection about the relation of man to his natural environment. Today we have the affluence to choose between orderly, well-conceived development of our total environment or the ill-planned cities, diminished natural resources, congested highways, and polluted water and air which in too many instances reflect our present land ethic.

Mr. Schmoe's book would be valuable for anyone who might wish to consider his own relationship and responsibility to a land so richly endowed with natural wealth and beauty.

— JOHN A. TOWNSLEY
Superintendent, Mount Rainier National Park, 1968

winter

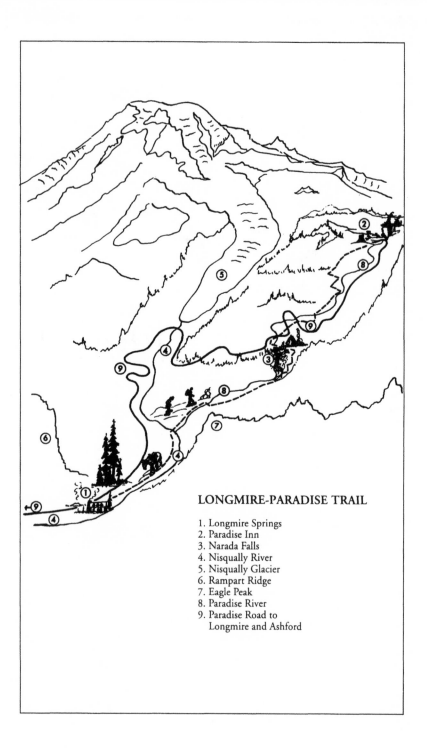

LONGMIRE-PARADISE TRAIL

1. Longmire Springs
2. Paradise Inn
3. Narada Falls
4. Nisqually River
5. Nisqually Glacier
6. Rampart Ridge
7. Eagle Peak
8. Paradise River
9. Paradise Road to
   Longmire and Ashford

1

WE WERE STRUGGLING UP A SNOWY incline from Longmire Springs to Paradise Inn, my wife Ruth and I. "Come on, dear," I called. "It's just over the next ridge." She was too exhausted to protest, and besides she had begun to realize that we would freeze to death if we remained much longer on the trail.

She was a small girl, although sturdily built. Even in her bulky winter clothing she appeared tiny and a bit pathetic to me that cold midwinter day on Mount Rainier.

This was our honeymoon, in a manner of speaking—a honeymoon long delayed because of the war. (The First World War that was—strange how already I begin to confuse the two.)

No one could deny that it was a hard trail even under the best of conditions and just here it was so steep that we wished we had snowshoes for our hands as well as our feet so that we could climb on all fours. I had been over the trail the week before but then it was well marked and Ranger Barnett had broken trail for me all the way. This was Ruth's first trip and her first encounter with snowshoes. Moreover, there was a foot or more of new snow and the old track was entirely blotted out.

Snowshoeing—certain misguided informants to the contrary—is definitely not a sport to be enjoyed for sport's sake. At best it is a means of travel through brush or over terrain too rugged for skis, where the snow is too deep and too soft to hold a man's weight. At its worst it is pure unmitigated torture.

Today it was torture even for me. It seemed that ten pounds of the sticky stuff clung to each web as we lifted it and that already we had picked up each foot with its heavy boot and heavier snowshoe at least ten thousand times to set it down again but a few inches above and beyond the last. Our legs, and especially those lifting muscles in the front of them that we never knew we had, were so sore that to touch them was painful and to take another step was agony. It began to seem that it might be better just to lie down in the soft fluffy snow and die.

But we had to go on. Paradise Inn *might* be just over the next ridge and for Ruth's sake I sincerely hoped that it was. She tells me now that that ridge was at least the seventh or eighth that we had climbed over, and that there were so many more yet to come that she cannot remember the actual number. Her memory may perhaps exaggerate things somewhat.

Again I said, "Come on, we *must* go," and I told her to be thankful that she had to lift only one foot at a time—but my attempt at humor did not bring even a weak smile to her tired face.

2

I HAD RETURNED FROM EUROPE only six months before, and after I had recovered somewhat from a siege of malarial fevers, we were married. We had gone directly to the University of Washington at Seattle. I wanted to continue my work in forestry and Ruth, who already had her degree in music, enrolled for some additional work in liberal arts. This was late in September of 1919.

Neither of us had been able to save any money during the years our marriage had been delayed by the war, and the *arbeit* I had always depended upon to pull me through simply did not "pull" hard enough for two. The cold fact was that two, with or without love, could not live as cheaply as one. By Christmas that year we were flat broke, and at least one of us had to drop out of school and get a job.

In the College of Forestry I knew a fellow who worked summers on Mount Rainier as a mountain guide. He told me that it was pleasant and exciting work, and that the pay was good. This last was important.

At that time I had never been on the huge old volcanic peak. I saw it the first morning we arrived in Seattle. It was a crisp, clear autumn morning, and the white mountain seemed to stand at the foot of Second Avenue just beyond the forty-two-story Smith Tower. I thought: *the first time I get a day off I'm going to hike out there.* We went immediately to the university. From the campus, Mount Rainier stood even higher, and I could see that there were foothills beyond Lake Washington and great forest, then the glaciers and the high summit. I realized then that it would be a long hike, *perhaps I could only walk to the base of the mountain and return in one day.* I was amazed when I discovered that it took four hours by train to reach even the edge of the National Park which surrounds the mountain.

But I had already made up my mind that I wanted to live on this mountain and work in the National Park, so now that we must have a job I decided to try to become a guide also.

I had had little experience with any mountains. I was a farm boy just come from the wheat fields of Kansas where, as some cynic has said, "You can see farther and see less than anywhere." Naturally I was vastly impressed by the great stands of timber, the wide blue lakes, and the rugged snowcapped peaks reaching high into the clouds of this Puget Sound country. I am still vastly impressed by them. But that this is a relative matter and that the cynics are seldom right was taught me by my father some years later when, for the first time, he visited us on the mountain. When I took him to a vantage point and showed him the huge peak which filled half the northern sky, he looked for a time, then turned to me and said, "It's beautiful, but what's it good for?" He was a wheat farmer.

While on a furlough in the French Alps I had had a bit of climbing experience and I hoped that I might talk my way into a job as a guide. If I could and if the pay was as good as my friend said that it was, we could return to school the next fall. This also was important, for I had already missed more than two years of college and I began to feel that old age was creeping up on me. I was then twenty-four!

So one day in December I went down to Coleman Dock and boarded the ancient Puget Sound steamer *Virginia II* for Tacoma. From the dock in Tacoma I walked uptown to the offices of the Rainier National Park Company, which is a private corporation operating the hotel, transportation, and guide services for the National Park. I asked General Manager T. H. Martin for a job as a company guide.

Actually, I knew next to nothing about being a guide, but it just so happened, as it sometimes does to needy mortals, that a chain of circumstances was all set up like apple blossoms in spring when the slightest touch will cause all the petals to fall in a shower. My name was German (but could be Swiss); I casually mentioned "some climbing experience in the Alps"; they had employed a professional Swiss guide the season before who had turned out to be an exceptionally good guide and an attractive and colorful character as well; I was a six-footer in good physical shape; travel to the National Parks was increasing following the war years. . . . "Yes," Mr. Martin said, "we will need some additional guides and you look like you might do." So the petals fell and I was hired on the spot.

But there was still another problem. The climbing season would not begin for six months, and if two healthy young people were to continue to eat in the manner to which they had become accustomed, I had to have some kind of a paying job right now.

T. H. Martin had the answer. He said there was an unusually heavy snowfall this winter and the National Park Inn at Longmire Springs was already sagging under the weight of it. If I was willing he would like to have me go up the very next day and start shoveling snow off the roof. "If somebody don't get the damn stuff off pretty soon the whole joint will cave in on us," he said.

The *Virginia II* was too slow for me. I took the train back to Seattle with my good news. We were already living on borrowed money and our Quaker consciences were bearing down on us like the snow on National Park Inn. The news I carried was a tremendous prop under that burden of worry.

I left by train early next morning for the mountain.

Within a week the next petal fell. Mr. Martin telephoned me at Longmire Springs: the insurance company required that a skeleton winter crew be kept at each of the National Park inns. The two men at Paradise Inn, thirteen miles by road or seven miles by trail farther up the mountain, had become bored to the point of brewing a batch of prune brandy and had been mad drunk for a week. This alcoholic state of affairs, he told me, had been hinted at by a number of maudlin telephone calls from Paradise during the first few days of the binge, and then followed by several days of complete and fearsome silence. The climax had come that very morning with the appearance in Tacoma of one of the men, badly mauled but not yet quite sober, on his way out of the park—and the company's service. His partner, condition unknown, was still unaccounted for. They had not been able to reach anyone at the inn by telephone. Mr. Martin asked me if I would like to return to Seattle for Ruth and go back to Paradise Inn immediately as the new winter keepers.

I threw my shovel off the roof and was in Seattle by evening.

Ruth was delighted, for she did not relish being left alone in Seattle. It was a better arrangement for the Park Company as well, for with a man and wife they got two people (thereby fulfilling the requirements of the insurance company) for almost the price of one. They would pay Ruth fifty dollars a month to cook for me.

3

MR. MARTIN BEAMED ON US the next day as we passed through Tacoma on our way to the mountain and in parting said, "I predict that if you two kids survive this winter alone in Paradise you will live happily together for the rest of your lives and go to heaven when you die." Then he told us that Paradise Inn was *completely buried under thirty feet of snow and that each of its hundred or more rooms was as dark as midnight even on the brightest day!*

Gus Anderson, who with his wife Olga was the winter keeper at National Park Inn, met us with a team and bobsled at Ashford. Ashford is a store and a service station at the end of a logging railroad fourteen miles below Longmire Springs and well outside the park. There was already three feet of snow at Ashford and about eight at Longmire.

On the long ride in, Gus told us something about the history of the area. The National Park was established in 1899 to protect the scientific and recreational values of this greatest of American mountains with its living glaciers and magnificent forests. The first wagon road was built by James Longmire and his sons in the 1880s, and it had been improved and extended to Paradise Valley in 1916. James Longmire had staked a mineral claim to include a series of warm mineral springs at the point now called Longmire Springs. He had also built the first hotel there, a ponderous log building, which stood until destroyed by fire in 1910. Two sons of James Longmire, Ben and Len, who were already legendary in their own right, still lived in the area. They had scouted and built most of the trails in the park, and Ben, who was of a romantic turn, had given most of the place-names to the minor attractions of the park.

Ben favored such names as *Fairy* Falls, *Mystic* Lake, *Fryingpan* Glacier, and *Fisher's Hornpipe* Creek. When in his explorations or trail-blazing he found a new stream or lake he simply thought up a name for it, carved it on a cedar shake split from a log, and nailed it to a tree. When the United States Geological Survey crews came in after the establishment of the National Park to survey and map the mountain, they put most of Ben's names on their maps. Later we came to know the Longmire boys well and from them heard many an exciting tale about the "old days" on the mountain.

Olga Anderson, mopping her plain round face now cherry-red from the hot kitchen range, met us at the door and helped Ruth out of her blankets and coats.

Paradise Inn in midwinter with thirty feet of snow on the ground and drifts a hundred feet deep. (Photo by L. D. Lindsley)

Paradise Inn as it appeared in the summer of 1922, with Pinnacle Peak and the Castle in the Tatoosh Range beyond. (Photo by L. D. Lindsley)

She was a big woman as blonde and as effervescent as Gus was dark and taciturn, and there was no question as to the sincerity of her welcome. Winters were long and lonely on the mountain. We quickly discovered also that she was a very good cook whose greatest joy was to have her guests display a liking for her meals by gorging themselves to capacity. She had a huge dinner ready for us, the central dish of which was a bear meat roast with browned potatoes and gravy.

There were only two rangers on the south side of the park at the time: quiet, scholarly, silver-haired J. B. Flett, a former professor of botany, who lived alone in a small cabin near the inn and who had dinner with us that night; and Herm Barnett, an old mountain man who lived with his family in the entrance lodge at the park boundary halfway between Longmire and Ashford. The bear meat came from Ranger Barnett, who had shot the animal at his back door (outside the park, since his cabin was at the park boundary).

4

MAYBE IT SHOULDN'T BE TOLD even now, for it was illegal, but in those days some of the rangers in outlying stations even had venison, grouse, and wild pigeon to eat. As Ben Longmire said, "If a big cock grouse attacks a body on the trail, a body's got to defend hisself, ain't he?"

Next morning Gus suggested that Ruth ride one of the horses as far as the Nisqually Crossing. The trail, he said, was fairly easy as far as the crossing and the snow was hard underneath, so it seemed like a good idea. It would leave her in better shape for the long pull at the upper end. We had breakfast before daybreak and Gus had "Brownie" saddled and ready at the door. Brownie and Whitie were the team which had made the hard twenty-eight-mile trip to Ashford the day before with the bobsled. It was only three miles to the crossing and then four miles by trail on up to Paradise Inn, but Paradise Inn was four thousand feet higher than Longmire Springs and the snow got deeper by the foot. Still we figured that with the early start and with Brownie to help us part way we would make the valley soon after noon, so we took only a couple of sandwiches for lunch along the way. At Narada Falls cabin, only a mile below the inn, we could have a fire and brew some tea and we hoped to eat our lunch there.

We tied Ruth's snowshoes and my pack behind the saddle, and Ruth mounted Brownie. The big bay horse was broad-backed and sturdy-legged and he looked capable enough. The Andersons bid us good-bye and asked us to be sure and call them the minute we arrived at the inn.

We followed the single wire of the government telephone line which stretched from tree to tree, I breaking trail and Ruth on Brownie close behind. We started out slow and easy for I knew it was a long, hard trail.

In the woods the old snow was not so hard as it was in the open and combined with the foot of fluffy new snow it made very difficult going. We soon discovered that it was harder on the horse than on us. In fact, Brownie floundered so badly in the belly-deep snow that Ruth had great trouble staying aboard and before we had gone a mile we decided to send him back. Gus had told us that he would return to the stable without trouble and that they would watch for him. So we tied his stirrups up, removed his bridle, and lashed it with a note to the saddle. We turned him around in the trail and headed him toward Longmire with a good-bye slap on his big fat rump. He seemed very much relieved to be returning home.

I shouldered the fifty-pound pack with our clothing and personal belongings, helped Ruth lash on her "bear paws" and we again started up the trail. From there on it would be simply a matter of slogging along . . . "pick 'em up and set 'em down," as Ben said . . . , climb ten minutes and rest five . . . , and beyond the river the trail got steeper and the snow deeper.

But it was quiet in the woods and wonderfully beautiful. After the storm of the night, the day had cleared and the sun, low in the south, was bright if not warm. Here in the silence of the great forest rays of light filtered through the crown of trees high above us and cast heavy shadows on the snow. To Ruth, who had never seen forests or mountains before, it was beyond description and she squeezed my arm to her side to express her feeling. To me it was like the long rays of light slanting down from the high windows in the nave of Notre Dame cathedral in Paris where I had often stopped to meditate and to rest, but this was a whiter, brighter cathedral than any built by man. The snowflakes which drifted lazily down from the branches above sparkled with a brilliance vastly greater than was ever caught by the motes of dust drifting about in the cathedral of Our Lady of Paris.

5

I KNEW THIS TYPE OF FOREST WELL, having cruised timber with forest engineering classes in similar areas around Seattle during the autumn term at the university, and I described the nature of it to Ruth whenever we stopped to rest. (I had learned that you go farther if you do not talk while climbing, and Ruth was already finding it difficult to talk and walk at the same time.)

Now we were deep in the Nisqually Valley somewhere between three and four thousand feet above sea level on the south side of the peak. Mount Rainier, being a dormant volcano of recent origin, has no direct relationship to the Cascade Mountains and stands well to the west of the main range—entirely within the Pacific slope drainage basin. Warm winds which have traveled for thousands of miles across the surface of the Pacific Ocean lift over the west slope of the Cascades, and strike the cold upper regions of the mountain peaks. Thus, most of their moisture is precipitated on the western slopes and on isolated Mount Rainier. They must lift to only six or seven thousand feet to flow over the Cascades, which stand only half as high as lofty Rainier, so most of the snowfall (and 75 percent of the annual precipitation is snowfall) comes to the lower slopes of the mountain. However, the summit reaches so high into the cold upper air that there is very little melting above seven thousand feet even during summer months, so the snow which does fall at the higher elevations remains to become ice and eventually flows down the sides of the mountain as glacial rivers.

At one time these glaciers extended all the way down to join the ice of the Puget Sound lobe of the great icecap. This was during the "recent" ice ages (some twenty-five thousand years ago). Since the retreat of the icecap, the local glaciers have also been melting back steadily, leaving behind these deep canyons and rushing rivers, and a fourteen-thousand-foot mountain peak which looks like the stump of a huge old tree with buttressed roots flaring out in all directions from its base. Eagle's Peak soaring two thousand feet almost vertically above us at this point and Rampart Ridge half as high on the other side of the canyon were buttresses of the old stump.

A few miles farther up the valley we would cross the Nisqually River, which now lay muffled under deep snow on our right. At the Nisqually Crossing we would see the rounded snow dome which is the terminus of the Nisqually Glacier and the birthplace of the river. This was the point on the mountain to which the great glaciers had receded so far; a point where, for the time being at least, a state of equilibrium had been established between snowfall and snow melt, between advancing ice and retreating ice.

Here in the dark damp canyon on the mild Pacific slope of the high Cascades grows one of the most luxuriant Temperate Zone forests known any place on earth. Rough-barked Douglas fir trees, some of them ten feet in diameter, stand close together and soar two to three hundred feet into the air. Ecologists call this the "Humid Transition Zone" forest, and we had been traveling through it from the time we had left Seattle early the day before. Below Ashford, where Gus had met us with the bobsled, there was considerable logging, and this was the occasion for the railroad which terminated at Ashford. Above the railroad was National Forest land surrounding the National Park, and here the forest was unbroken except for the ribbons cut by roaring rivers and the islands formed by rocky peaks.

In winter the entire world is muffled by heavy blankets of snow. Now it was fresh, new snow, and although tons of it weighed down the treetops high above us and it was constantly slipping off overweighted branches and falling in silver showers among the trees, it was not dangerous to us. Later in the winter, especially during sudden thaws following heavy snowfalls, great masses of wet snow would fall with a constant thud, thud, thud, in the forest, and then it would be unsafe to travel on deep forest trails such as these.

Yesterday, bundled under warm robes in the bed of the sleigh and again today on the trail, we looked up in wonder and amazement at the ragged bits of sky which we could see among the treetops high above us. Even when the sun shines, the floor of this forest is kept in a deep and brooding twilight.

But in this forest, with all its prolific and luxuriant growth, there is in fact a limited number of species. This applies to both plants and animals and is a result of the heavy shade. Most plants and animals, like men, love the sun and thrive best in its warm rays. Comparatively few have adapted themselves to a shade environment. Here the Douglas fir, one of America's finest lumber-producing trees, hogs all the sunshine. As a species it refuses to grow in shade, even in the shade of its parent trees, and it has somehow managed to overtop all other species so that it does not need to do so. Except for occasional marshy areas too wet for its air-breathing roots, it dominates the lower slopes and valleys, so that in looking down upon it from a height you see an unbroken carpet of dark green trees with even darker ribbons here and there where alders and cottonwoods border a stream, and mottled patches where yellow-green cedars flourish in the marshy areas. Frequently these wet areas are the work of a family of industrious beavers who have dammed a small stream to make a safe home for themselves and a millpond for their logging operations. This pond eventually grows up with aquatic plants and then silts in and in time becomes a swamp or a marshy meadow, where later still the huge western red cedar will grow.

If forest life here is not greatly varied, as it is in the Temperate Zone forests farther east, it is vastly more abundant. First, as I pointed out to Ruth, there is an understory of shade-loving (or rather shade-tolerant) trees. These are mostly western hemlocks, only a bit less tall and majestic than the Douglas firs, and a scattering of lovely silver firs and clean-boiled white pines. These trees are "ladies in waiting" in a very real sense. They are waiting for the time when they may be able to grasp the sunshine and dominate the forest. For trees, like people, have a fairly definite age limit after which they become decadent and die—or being weakened by age and senility they fall easy victim to wind, fire, insect, or fungus disease. These dominantly Douglas fir forests, since they started as seedlings in open areas caused by blowdown or fire, are likely, in a given site or area, to be all of about the same age. So they reach their age limit (their "three score and ten," as it were) all at about the same time and then begin to fall out. If at this peak of their lives, at this "climax" of the stand, they are cut by the logger, blown down by the wind, or fall victim to a forest fire, other firs will spring up like grass from the millions of seeds that have accumulated in the duff of the forest floor, and the typical Douglas fir forest will succeed itself. But if, as often happens, there is no woodsman's ax, no great catastrophe of nature or sweeping epidemic of insect or disease to wipe the forest clean, the ancient veterans fall out when their time comes one by one and this understudy of hemlock, silver fir, and pine very quickly takes over. For a season the forest will be more varied, since the dominant Douglas fir has for the moment lost control.

This condition never lasts long, for where the old-age limit of the fir is around eight hundred to a thousand years, that of the hemlock, the pine, and the silver fir is only about half as long. So they, like the fir, go "the way of all flesh" and may or may not succeed themselves, depending upon the circumstances of their passing.

Since the Douglas fir is the preferred species for commercial uses, the forester takes advantage of this sun-loving trait and cuts his woodland clean, then burns the slash leaving great scars of black upon the mountainside. The casual visitor and sightseer is shocked by this apparent ruthlessness and loudly protests the logger's methods, but modern Paul Bunyan knows what he is doing. If he can protect his cut-over area from the careless fires of these same protesting visitors, he will in a very short time get a dense new growth of tall straight seedlings that are almost 100 percent Douglas firs. In a short forty years he will again have a maximum production of merchantable timber. If, on the other hand, he used a selective rather than a clean-cutting method (which would be the right thing to do in a mixed or hardwood forest), he would do just what nature sometimes does by allowing trees to fall out one by one leaving their places to be taken immediately by the waiting hemlocks and other inferior (commercially speaking) species.

In the swampy areas the cedars, which hang on to life like Methuselah, and often grow to be fifteen hundred years of age, and as large, if not as tall, as the Douglas firs, maintain the *status quo* over longer periods. But even here the nature of the forest is in constant change. Eventually the swamp will be drained and the soil dry out. The cedar seedlings will no longer germinate in the dry soil, and eventually the Douglas fir may take over even the former swamp. Four hundred miles to the south, the California redwood plays a similar role in another magnificent West Coast forest.

Underneath the giant trees on the floor of the forest there is a fascinating community of shade-tolerant plants and animals. Most of the plants which make up the flora of this community were now buried deep under the snow, but where our trail passed through swamps at the edge of the river, and especially in the yarding areas of the bands of deer where the hungry, snowbound animals had trampled paths and beds in the snow, we could see some of the heavy-spined devil's-club, the evergreen salal and Oregon grape, and the masses of deer and sword fern which make up the bulk of the rough ground cover in these dark forests. Not until the spring thaws removed the overburden of snow could we find the delicate shamrock-like sorrel, the saprophytic barber pole, coral cup and Indian pipe, and the masses of bleeding heart and vanilla leaf which would carpet the spaces between the moss-covered logs and the clumps and thickets of tall fern fronds. There would be snow-white, wax-petaled anemones, trillium and huckleberry, Canadian dogwood also in the deep forests, and in secret spots, occasional clumps of the lovely purple and red lady's slipper calypso orchids.

These are only the conspicuous forest plants to be set off by a mass of conservative mosses, lichens, and fungus plants which form the ground color on tree trunks, fallen logs, stones, and hang from even the smallest branches clear up to the towering tips of the trees themselves. Only in the very darkest recesses of the forest would the background colors change from the green of growing plants to the browns of dead leaves, needles, fallen twigs, decaying wood, and the other debris of a forest floor. But all these, including the invisible bacteria, the minute fungus plants, the insects, worms, and larger animals, have a vital part in the reduction of the forest litter to soil from which new growth can spring and so are part of the great wheel which must swing down in death in order to swing up again in life and so roll across the face of time and space.

And this is all one community, all parts intimately related, each part engaged in a strange, but wonderful, "co-operative competition" within the whole.

Later I made forest ecology my major interest, and I learned much more of the co-operative adjustments, the interrelationships, and the delicate balances which are not visible to even the most careful spectator in the forest but must rather be observed and learned through laboratory research, where with compound microscopes and a vast array of complicated measuring and analyzing devices the hidden inner secrets and the intimate life stories of the plants and animals are sought out. There is, for example, that strange marriage by which a tiny algae and a fungus plant blend their bodies into an entirely different plant called a lichen and live together to the mutual advantage of both, but reproduce separately as two entirely different plants. And there is the even more secret alliance between the nitrogen-fixing bacteria which set up little factories on the roots of the alder (as with the legumes) to provide food for themselves and soil nourishment for their host and their neighbors. There is a similar relationship between certain fungi and the roots of the Douglas fir (as with the orchids also) which is vastly profitable to the firs (and to the orchids) and presumably of value to the fungi as well.

In spite of all these individual members of this forest community (and hundreds of others unmentioned and even unseen), this is still a simple and a primitive forest compared to, say, a hardwood forest of the Eastern United States or Europe, where there are some five hundred species of trees alone compared to a mere thirty or forty varieties in a Pacific Coast coniferous forest.

It is fascinating to me, and Ruth also found it so, that these intimate relationships and associations, stemming in this case from the basic volcanic soil, the heavy moisture content of the mild-tempered Pacific winds, and the shade cast by the great trees, are so constant and so dependable that a trained forester or biologist should be able, if set down alongside any given species of tree, to take a quick look around and tell you with considerable accuracy the elevation, the normal rainfall, the temperature ranges, and the names of most of the associated plants and animals to be found in that vicinity.

6

AT THE NISQUALLY CROSSING, where the bridge was entirely lost under the snow, we passed over the river and after an exhausting scramble emerged out of the canyon into an area entirely unlike the lower forest. This to the ecologist is the "Canadian Zone."

We were in this open woods at noon and still far below the Narada cabin, but I did not know exactly where we were. The new snow which had fallen since my first trip over the trail had changed the looks of the countryside. Then the mountain was clear and there had been a well-packed track. Now again the mountain had drawn her veil of clouds and assumed the role of a modest virgin. Even the telephone line, which was the only mark of man we had left, conspired to confuse us. In this more open country it often took short cuts across canyons or up rock cliffs whereas we had to go around. In places also the low-slung wire was completely buried under the deep snow.

I was thinking of these things as we ate our meager lunch alongside the trail, but kept my worries to myself. The rest and food revived us somewhat and we struggled on up the mountainside.

The dense lower-slope forests of fir and hemlock had been moody and silent. A few Oregon jays had followed us out of Longmire Springs, but they soon left us and returned to the clearings. Even the swift-flowing Nisqually River, which roars and grinds all spring and summer, was hushed by the cold and blanketed under the snow. We talked in low tones, for there is something about the deep quiet of the woods that calms and quiets people. Except for the blue jays and ravens, who are alway raucous, it seems that even the birds and the animals are influenced by this somber mood of the deep woods. I often noticed this later in the year when I would ski swiftly down the silent trail and drop suddenly from the bright and happy alpine meadows into the somber forest. The silence seemed to bear in on me just as the trees closed in on the trail. And we noticed it this day in reverse, as some hours later we climbed out of the forested foothills and into the brighter and freer atmosphere of the high, open valleys.

As I have said, the change comes with dramatic suddenness. At an elevation of about 4,500 feet we stepped out into the brightness of a small, open area. Beyond we could see other openings, and along the flat summit of Mazama Ridge, now in sight about a mile beyond us, there were only small clumps of trees here and there like wooded islands in a sea of snow. These open areas, with the ground still buried under twenty feet of snow, were the beginning of the broad alpine meadows so characteristic of Mount Rainier. Few of the other American peaks have them, although they are characteristic of the Swiss Alps. During the brief spring and summer the snow melts away and these mountain meadows burst into such a gorgeous display of wild flowers as to be totally unimaginable to us on that winter day. We were both near exhaustion but this sudden release from the forest cheered and revived us.

Suddenly we felt very much at home in this parklike Eden above the somber lower-slope forests. Here where there were light and space and love, life renewed itself. I pushed back my parka hood, took Ruth's cold face in my hands, and gently kissed her. It warmed us both.

7

WHAT FOREST ECOLOGISTS CALL THE Canadian Zone (comparing it with that almost unbroken band of dense coniferous forest which extends across all the land areas of the Northern Hemisphere in the latitude of Canada, and which produces the bulk of the pulpwood consumed by the newspapers of the world) is here on Mount Rainier really a transition zone—the narrow overlap between the Humid Transition Zone with its somber forest of huge trees, and the freer Hudsonian Zone, an area of open meadows, bare ridges, and glacial lakes which we were now entering.

Around the world spruce is the key tree of the Canadian Zone, and we had noted an occasional Sitka spruce along the trail, but here in the high Cascades noble fir *(Abies nobilis*)* is its true index. Ruth and I had climbed through an almost pure stand of these beautiful trees along the upper Nisqually River. The tiny bunchberry dogwood, whose species name is *canadensis,* is also characteristic of this zone but not entirely confined to it as the noble fir is.

*Now revised to *Abies procera.*

Practical woodsmen like Ben and Len Longmire, and even explorers like Lewis and Clark, feel that they must give names to their new discoveries because a name is a sort of a handle by which they can present these things in their stories or describe them in their reports. A strictly new name is, it seems, something very hard to come up with on the spur of the moment. Even the scientists, who usually fall back upon their knowledge of Latin and Greek to build new names by combining descriptive terms from one or both of those languages, often do almost as badly as the woodsmen who are without benefit of classic languages.

The easiest thing to do always is to call a new plant or animal by the name of the known plant or animal that it most nearly resembles, or appears to resemble, in the eyes of its discoverer. So to Captain Vancouver, looking over the endless coniferous forests that crowded the shores of Puget Sound for as far as he could see, these were "pines," and the first Douglas fir lumber exported from Astoria, Oregon, by the Hudson Bay Company was sold as "Oregon pine." On Asian markets it is today still sold as Oregon pine.

The botanist Menzies, who accompanied Vancouver, examined this species unknown to Europe and knew that it was not a true pine, but he had no name for it. Some twenty-five years later the Scottish botanist David Douglas was sent out by the Royal Horticultural Society to examine and describe the new tree. He called it "a sort of hemlock" and later the French botanist Carrière, who had never seen the tree, came up with the genus name of *Pseudotsuga* and added the species name *taxifolia*. By now the matter of Vancouver's new "pine" was thoroughly confused. It was, to give it its full technical name, Douglas fir *(Pseudotsuga taxifolia)*. To anyone able to read in five languages it was "David Douglas' fir, the false hemlock with the yewlike leaves"—"Douglas" presumably being Scottish, "fir" English, *"Pseudo"* Greek, *"tsuga"* Japanese, and *"taxi"* and *"folia"* both Latin. And in spite of all this confusion it is *not* a fir, nor yet a hemlock, and the leaves do not closely resemble those of the yew. Recently foresters have fairly well agreed to change the species name to *menzieseii*, but they let the common name stand. To change that would upset the lumber markets of the world and mystify loggers and lumber merchants still further.

Actually, the only trees which should be called "fir" are the balsams of the genus *Abies*, the "Tannenbaum" of the Germans, of which there are four species found in the park. Of these four *true* firs, noble fir is the most impressive because of its size and symmetry, and alpine fir *(Abies lasiocarpa)*, which is characteristic of the high parklands we were just entering, the most beautiful. The two other species—silver fir *(Abies amabilis,* meaning "lovely") and lowland white fir *(Abies grandis)*—are also magnificent trees. These latter two species grow as occasional specimens scattered throughout the lower-slope forests.

8

FARTHER UP IN THE VALLEY WE FOUND that alpine firs and mountain hemlocks dominated the landscape completely and grew singly, or in small clumps scattered over the open meadows. The Alaska cedar, reduced here to the size of a shrub, grew only in sheltered areas such as the small Edith Creek Canyon back of Paradise Inn. In the high country the rare beauty of the alpine trees was most apparent. The tall alpine firs reached skyward like Gothic spires, while the darker and more ragged mountain hemlocks fell into angular planes and points resembling Chinese pagodas. This day a heavy festoon of soft new snow lay heavily on all the trees and they were beautiful far beyond our meager powers of description.

Here wildlife appeared again as if, like us, it had suddenly been re-leased from the smothering grip of the deep woods. Chestnut-backed chickadees, ignoring us completely, worked the tips of twigs and branches for tiny insect eggs and larvae, small flocks of rosy finches dipped and swooped in close formations across the snowy meadows, and a few crowlike "nutcrackers" sat on the tips of the tallest trees and, cocking their heads sidewise, examined us minutely with their beady eyes. They did not seem at all suspicious of us but exhibited only a questioning sort of curi-osity, as though they were willing to wait with patience for us to explain our uninvited presence.

This "nutcracker," more often called Clark's crow here in the Pacific Northwest where he was first noted by that exploring team of Lewis and Clark, is actually a crow in everything except size and color. He is smaller than the crows, but larger than the jays, and he wears a modest habit of Quaker gray and black. This *habit,* however, is the only Quakerly thing about the lout, for he is a quarrelsome hijacker and robber who dominates the bird life of the high country and even tries to dictate to the animals. Later in the year we often saw and heard Clark's crow scolding bear and deer and even attacking squirrels and marmots.

Clark's crow, or nutcracker, one of the bold winter birds which came every morning to the kitchen window to be fed. This bird was first noted by the Lewis and Clark Expedition and is unique to the northwestern mountains. (Photo by Floyd Schmoe)

Like the redheaded California woodpecker, he stores food during lush seasons for the hungry winters. The woodpecker buries his acorns in holes which he drills for them in the bark of the oak trees, but the lazy nutcracker simply stashes his food in little caches among the densely matted branches of the alpine trees.

Ruth had never before seen this bold highland bandit, since he never, even in the coldest winters, comes into the lowlands around Puget Sound. I remembered him immediately from a dramatic maneuver he had demonstrated for me one time high in the Montana Rockies. I had been climbing above timberline and had stopped on a high rocky ridge to rest and admire the view. The sheer canyon wall dropped for a thousand feet or more below me. I had been noticing the birds as I climbed, and especially these big fellows because they were so bold and because I had never seen them before and did not know their habits. So I was amazed when two of them, who had been sitting in some timberline trees near my resting place and observing me critically, suddenly flew out over the canyon, paused a moment in mid-air, then closed their wings and plummeted like falling stones for a thousand feet to the bottom of the gorge. There they flattened out and disappeared from sight in the trees along the riverbank.

To the Clark's crows I am sure this was pure pastime . . . , a thriller staged for me but mostly for their own enjoyment. I could imagine them sitting on a branch far below me and saying to themselves: "I'll bet that knocked his eye out!"

9

IT WAS MIDAFTERNOON WHEN WE CAME at last to the ranger station at Narada Falls. We found dry fuel behind the stove and built a fire. There were blankets hung by wires from the rafters to keep them from the mice, but there was no food in the cupboards. Ruth collapsed on the bunk. I removed her snowshoes and boots and tried to call Gus at Longmire but the telephone was out of order.

For a long time I considered whether we should go on or stay at the cabin overnight without food. It is only a mile and a half by trail to Paradise Inn from Narada, but the trail is very steep. I felt we should stay for Ruth's sake, but I was afraid Gus and Olga would be worried when we did not check in and Gus might spend the night with the rangers looking for us. I decided to push on.

It took a great deal of will power for me to strap on the webs again and shoulder our pack. For Ruth it was sheer torture. During the hour's rest our legs had become so sore and stiff that they threatened to give way under us when we attempted to stand. I felt very sorry for Ruth. This was asking too much of a young girl who had lived most of her life in the city and was never what might be called the athletic or outdoor type anyway. But she was brave and willing to follow my judgment. Neither of us yet knew how long a mile and a half could be.

At Narada Falls the Paradise River leaps out of the high valley into the deep canyon. From here the road creeps back and forth in a series of steep switchbacks, but the trail climbs directly up the river, which leaps down a series of small waterfalls called the Washington Cascades. We could hear the rushing water under the heavy snow, and in places there were open holes over fast water which added a real hazard to the trail.

Above these falls we were in the valley proper. The term "valley" is somewhat misleading. Although it is a typical "hanging valley" it is quite unlike what most of us think of when we use the term. Actually, Paradise Valley is a high bold shoulder of the mountain spreading flat on either side of the Paradise River but still surrounded on three sides by great ridges. Paradise Inn is perched on a narrow shelf halfway up the left-hand ridge.

Like Sunset Park, Indian Henry's Hunting Ground, Yakima Park, and the other lovely alpine meadows of Mount Rainier, it is the floor of a glacial cirque. Above its headwall lies the broad expanse of the Paradise ice fields and here the Paradise River, newborn in the icy caverns of the glacier, emerges to plunge immediately over the headwall into the valley. This is Sluiskin Falls, where the Cowlitz Indian guide, Sluiskin, waited fearfully while Stevens and Van Trump made their first successful ascent of the mountain in August of 1870. According to General Hazard Stevens, the Indian occupied his time hunting mountain sheep for food but in this, and in spite of his skill as a hunter and the abundance of "sheep," he was unsuccessful and settled for some fat marmots instead. Stevens' "sheep" were likely white mountain goats which are still abundant on the mountain, while mountain sheep are unknown in the area.

At Narada Falls the river dives two hundred feet down and out of the "valley" into a deep canyon which joins the Nisqually Canyon and River some miles below. What we call Paradise Valley is the high isolated benchland between these two falls.

Here at last our trail came out into entirely open country with nothing apparently between us and the summit of the mountain yet some ten miles away. The great white dome now and again unveiled by drifting clouds towered nine thousand feet above us and seemed almost to hang over us. We were two tiny black dots on a great white field and we were looking at a view which, although we were too tired to enjoy it, neither of us will ever forget.

But the hotel was still nowhere in sight, although I knew that it could not be far beyond. Actually it was dusk of the short winter day before it finally came into view. All that we saw were a few feet of the two massive stone chimneys protruding from a mound in the endless expanse of snow.

It was, however, a most welcome sight! Ruth dropped in a heap in the soft snow and I could hear her crying in relief and exhaustion.

Even yet it looked a long way off, although we were almost upon it before I had seen it in the gathering dusk.

It was hard to realize that these chimneys, from which no welcoming smoke appeared, were in fact forty feet tall and that a huge three-story building lay buried in the drifts below them. This "hole in the ground," this rabbit warren in the snow, was to be our home—our "honeymoon cottage" for the rest of the long winter. Still it looked very good to me that day on the trail.

The telephone line had completely disappeared again under the snow. Since Narada Falls, our only guide had been "up." Now we had arrived. In another fifteen minutes we were at the entrance to a tunnel which sloped sharply downward to a *second-story* door. We were home, and only just in time. The night would soon be black and the temperature was already well below zero.

We pounded on the door at the end of the dark tunnel and waited, but there was no response. The door was unlocked. I opened it and we went in. The stove was cold, there was no sign of life. This worried us, for we expected to find one member of the winter crew still on the job. We knew that there had been a fight and that only one man had shown up in Tacoma. We wondered if perhaps there might have been murder in Paradise.

10

ON THE WAY UP WE HAD SEEN no down tracks at any place. The snowfall of the night had presumably stopped at daybreak as it had at Longmire. We hoped at first that our unknown friend had taken a short cut down and so evaded us on the trail, but there was now the uneasy feeling that, dead or alive, he was still somewhere in the dark catacombs of the hotel. Ruth lay down on a couch, too fatigued and too relieved at having finally reached shelter to be frightened or worried. I quickly found matches and lighted a fire in the big living room stove. Then I got the boots off her numb feet and wrapped her in a blanket. She was already sound asleep. I found a lantern and started a room-to-room search of the hotel. Counting kitchens, pantries, storerooms, and public rooms, there were more than a hundred rooms to examine. After an hour of fruitless search my fears increased and I called Gus at Longmire Springs. There was still a large room in the basement that was fastened with a padlock.

Gus and Olga were very much worried about us. Brownie had returned in good shape with our note, and they had been waiting all day to hear from us. They were about ready to report us missing to Ranger Barnett.

Gus had no solution to the problem of the second man. No person had passed by that they had seen and, so far as Herm knew, no one had gone out through the entrance gate. They too thought our man was still in Paradise (we hoped it was Paradise Valley). Gus advised me to break down the locked door in the basement.

This room turned out to be the carpentry shop, and the dusty benches and tables indicated that it had not been used for months. I went over the entire hotel again and then, in spite of my aching legs, bundled up, put my snowshoes back on, went outside, and with the lantern made a careful search all around the building. I found no other openings and no tracks save those we had made shortly before.

Ruth was still sleeping, so I prepared a hot meal from canned food found on the pantry shelf. When it was ready I awakened her and we sat near the roaring stove to eat. The timbers of the huge building creaked and snapped under the weight of snow and the falling temperature. By late bedtime we had pretty well convinced ourselves that our elusive friend must have left before dawn, missing us on the trail, and that the snow which might have fallen longer in Paradise Valley than at Longmire Springs had covered his tracks. If this were true, he had also skirted the inn at Longmire and slipped through the gate at the park entrance without alerting anyone. In this case he would have had to make the entire twenty-eight miles to Ashford in one day and all of it through new snow. It was a very long hike for a man with a hangover even though it was all downhill! I turned my thoughts to other things. This was becoming more of an adventure than we had anticipated. I could endure it but what of Ruth? For the first time I began to wonder if we had done the right thing in taking this job—if I had done right in bringing her into this vast desolation of snow and silence.

I had met her years before when we were both in high school in a Kansas town. We were farm-born, both from small Quaker communities in the eastern part of the state. Later she lived in the city and I had come there because there was no high school in our rural area. I was living with an uncle and an aunt. After high school I stayed on for a year at the local Friends college just to be near her, although I had already settled on my profession and knew that the work I could get at this little Midwest college would not help me much in forestry.

At the end of that year we were engaged. She was only seventeen. We knew it would be a long time before we could marry. Europe was at war. America was becoming involved. Draft laws were in prospect. I was twenty.

And I still had four or five years of university ahead.

I never really asked her to marry me. I said, as I remember, "Darling, I love you very much. Do you think that someday you could be my wife?" Her arms around my neck and her head on my breast said "Yes" enough. When I walked home to my dormitory room later that night I am sure that my feet never once touched the ground.

I had been walking on dreams ever since. During my next year at the College of Forestry of the University of Washington in Seattle the dream had expanded and grown, and even through the muck and suffering of the Meuse and the Marne, where I served with a volunteer ambulance unit, and later in the famine and fever of Poland, where I went with the Hoover Commission, it had not dimmed.

Ruth in the meantime, an accomplished pianist, was training for a concert career. It meant work and sacrifice for her mother, left a widow with four daughters to rear.

Now in midwinter in this desolate place I began to wonder if I had any right to take her away from a life suited to her talents and hide her in an uninhabited wilderness. True, she shared with me my love of beauty in nature, my awe and wonder of magnificent places. Her gentle nature and spirit made her kin to the gentle and lovely in flowers, trees, and shy wild things. But had I overenticed her with my stories? Now for the first time, I realized that my life as a forester would not be all sunshine and birds singing. Would she come to grieve for the life she had left: for the concert hall, the friends and the flowers and the applause? What did I offer her in their place? *My* ambitions? *My* success? Even my love and my children— would these be enough for her?

In spite of these doubts, I slept soundly all night, and would have no doubt even if the roof had caved in on us. I cannot remember any time in my life when I was more completely exhausted, except the time more than a year earlier when I had carried stretchers for forty-eight hours during the battle of Château-Thierry. The night following that ordeal I slept through an air raid in Paris while buildings were being knocked down in the next block.

11

NEXT DAY GUS REPORTED BY TELEPHONE to Tacoma that peace and sobriety had once more been established in Paradise. No one, so far as we ever learned, knew the answer to the riddle of the missing man. Fortunately for our peace of mind, we had not yet discovered the half-dozen or so other buildings in the valley. There was a ranger station, ranger's cabin, guidehouse, laundry, employees' dormitory, stables, and shops all completely buried under the snow. We never knew that most of them existed until suddenly they were exposed by the snow melting in the spring.

Our first day in Paradise was glorious. The sun was well above Mazama Ridge when we awoke and looked out. The saw-toothed Tatoosh Range, watched over by a stiff-backed little Matterhorn called Pinnacle Peak, guarded our southern boundary, and the soaring dome of the mountain, dazzling now in the horizontal rays of the winter sun, the gleaming névé snows set off by the deep shadows of the canyons, was a heavenly mansion big enough to fill the entire sky in the north and west. Not a breath of wind disturbed the calm and all the trees had tucked in their green skirts and covered themselves with deep-piled mantles of ermine.

Winter birds, we discovered that day, were all over the place, and there were signs of animals too, both indoors and out. These would keep us company in Paradise. We were both interested in birds and animals and since none of these seemed unfriendly or resentful of our intrusion, we welcomed them. This, we told ourselves, was not so much a Paradise of golden streets and pearly gates as a wintry Garden of Eden.

These four-footed neighbors quickly made themselves known to us. When I looked outside the door I found coyote tracks in the snow at the entrance to the tunnel. A stray dog coyote (by the size of his track) had been snooping around the skis and snowshoes stacked there. Perhaps it was only curiosity over the unfamiliar man scent, or possibly he was hungry enough to have considered eating the rawhide webs out of our snowshoes. Whatever was in his mind, he had presently gone off again and his tracks disappeared over the rim of the valley. We did not see him. Down the trail a way were the tracks of a bobcat or a lynx. Their round tracks, which do not show claw marks, are easily distinguished from the doglike tracks of a coyote or a wolf, but you cannot tell the two wild cats apart by their tracks. Both species, as well as the cougar or mountain lion, are numerous in the park.

This fellow obviously knew exactly where he was going, for he didn't stop to investigate, or even change his pace, when he crossed our deep trail of the previous evening. His precisely spaced pugs led straight as a bowstring across the meadows.

Near the foot of a large hemlock we saw where a marten had sprung about sixteen feet out into the snow—a tremendous leap for an animal smaller than a house cat—and then had run in great four-foot leaps to the next clump of trees. At that time I had never seen a marten, since they are peculiarly an animal of the high country, but the pairs of footprints side by side were sure indication of a member of the weasel tribe, and these footprints were three times the size of those of an ordinary ermine, or even those of a mink—and no mink would likely be so far from running water. Later we found that there were many marten in Paradise Valley and in similar areas around the mountain. Within the National Park they are not the shy and elusive animal trappers say they are. Sometimes they even came into the hotel and played around among the exposed beams and rafters of the barnlike hotel lobby. No animal, not even a monkey, is so sure-footed and fearless an aerialist. They are the only animals that can run down and catch a red squirrel in his native treetop. Red squirrels, unfortunately, seem to be their preferred meat, although in the alpine meadows where tree squirrels are few, the ground squirrel and the cony suffer most.

It was not this winter but another a few years later, when we had skied into Paradise Valley and spent Christmas with friends at Paradise Inn, that I saw the most beautiful little picture of wilderness life in all my experience. By then the inn had electricity even during the winter, and we had strung colored lights through the branches of a tall alpine fir just outside the dining room window. Heavy snow had fallen, weighting the tree down and burying the lights, but although the bulbs were hidden the colored lights shone through the snow, causing the entire Christmas tree to glow. On Christmas eve after dinner, we turned the lights off in the dining room and switched on the lights outside. A pair of martens were playing in the tree. They were startled for a moment but then, ignoring the lights and the spectators inside the window, they resumed their game of tag, chasing each other from limb to limb, up and down the tree. Occasionally they would stop and peer at us only a few feet away inside the window. Their eyes were bright in their pert little foxlike faces, but they were even quicker and more alert than foxes. We watched them fascinated for many minutes until they chased each other away into the clear, subzero night.

There are eight members of this bloodthirsty clan to be found on Mount Rainier, but not one of the other seven is as carefree and happy a buccaneer as the impish, bright-faced little marten. In order of size the family runs like this: Streator's "little" weasel (one of which I later caught in a mousetrap in Paradise Inn); the Washington weasel, which is the common "ermine" of the winter park; the little, spotted skunk, or polecat; the mink, a water lover or at least a water dweller because he prefers eating fish and frogs; the marten I have just described who is definitely arboreally inclined; his larger cousin with similar habits, the Pacific fisher, who so far as I know never goes fishing but seems to prefer to kill and eat the spiny porcupine instead of fish; the Pacific otter, who is a born swimmer and fisherman and as playful as the marten although he does not look so bright and happy; and the "gulo" or wolverine who is the largest and most destructive of all the weasels.

There are few wolverines left in the Northwest and few people regret their passing. With the disposition they have they could never be numerous in any area since they cannot tolerate even each other. I have never seen one free in the woods, but the destruction I have seen them wreak on a trapper's cabin causes me to think that bears are by comparison ideal neighbors. A wolverine no larger than a six-month-old cub could, I am sure, lick any pair of full-grown bears, and if they were as large as a bear nothing in the woods, including men, would be safe from them. The closest I ever knowingly came into contact with a wolverine was through the parka I wore. It was Eskimo-made, and the long, brown fur around the hood was wolverine fur. Eskimos use wolverine fur for this purpose because for some reason moisture from the breath does not form ice on wolverine fur in even the coldest weather.

12

ON CALM, BRIGHT MORNINGS, especially after a storm when nature seemed to catch her breath and start living again, I liked to go out to read the stories of the night's doings as it was written on the fresh white pages of the new snow. There would be hundreds of lacy trails made by mice, shrews, weasels, marten, and the winter birds, and often I found the marks of wings and talons in the snow where a mouse trail, and a mouse life, abruptly ended because a hungry hawk or owl was out and watching too.

Such a tragic incident all but happened inside our entrance tunnel late one sunny afternoon. I was sitting near the door and saw a shadow flash past the tunnel entrance. I got up and went to the tunnel and looked out. A sparrow hawk, perched in the tip of a nearby tree, had a disappointed look. I glanced down at my feet before turning back to the warmth of the house and saw a tiny shrew there on the snow. When I started to pick him up he snarled and hissed and put up such a belligerent front that I drew on a leather ski mitt before scooping him up and taking him inside. He had no appreciation for his rescue but kept squealing and tearing at my mitt with the rows of needle-sharp teeth in his beaklike mouth. This half-pint insectivore, who weighs a scant ounce when fully grown, is the smallest mammal known, and one of the most voracious. Someone has said that if the shrews—who live in the leaves and duff of both wooded and cultivated areas over most of North America from Mexico to well beyond the Arctic Circle, as well as in Europe, Asia, and Africa, but are still unseen and unknown by most people—were suddenly to grow as big as cats and dogs and at the same time retain their appetites in similar ratio, they would certainly wipe out all other wildlife on the continent—and in a matter of days.

Driven by an eternal hunger which must be like a smoldering fire in their vitals, they forage day and night, gorging on whatever falls prey to their search whether it is worm, insect, or carrion, and sleep only for minutes at a time upon a full stomach. When really hard-pressed for fuel to stoke the gastric flames, these minute crosses between a mouse, a wolf, and the devil will attack and kill birds and animals many times their size, and do not hesitate to defy a man or a dog. To keep life alive in their mad little bodies they kill and eat several times their own weight each day and if denied all food they will starve to death between daylight and dark.

I brought the big galvanized washtub into the living room and put our little gladiator into it for safekeeping and observation. He began immediately to dash about trying to escape, and when he found he could not climb the steep sides of his arena, he tried to gnaw a hole in the metal with his teeth. Completely frustrated he stood on his hind legs like a miniature kangaroo, gnashed his teeth, and squealed. Long after we had gone to bed I heard his tiny claws scratching at the metal tub and when I got up in the

The weasel and the snowshoe rabbit

morning he was dead. Petruchio and his friends would have had a jolly time taming this shrew.

Down in the lower woods on the Longmire trail when later I made weekly trips for mail and supplies, I would always find tracks of the big snowshoe rabbit, or as he is more correctly known, the varying hare. Once I witnessed a brief but bloody battle between a snowshoe rabbit and a weasel.

There was at the time about six inches of downy new snow on top of the denser, older snow. The white fluff was still falling lazily, as such snow does, and piling up on the ground like thistledown. The long-legged hare had no difficulty running in it, but when I saw them the rabbit was so befuddled and terrified by his deadly enemy that he could not run but only cowered in the snow, leaping a few feet aside when the weasel struck at him. The weasel, with legs only half as long as the rabbit's ears, could not run on the new snow at all so he ran *under* the fluffy stuff, leaping up now and then to look around as a dog does when he is hunting in high grass.

It was on the flat near the Springs, and I saw them first when the yellow-white weasel popped up out of the snow almost at my feet. He disappeared immediately and I stopped to look around. Then I saw the befuddled hare crouching in the snow. He was apparently expecting the little devil to pop up almost anywhere—which he did. The rabbit avoided him two or three times but he had no chance at all. At about the third or fourth try the weasel came up near enough to throw himself at the hare and sink his fangs into the rabbit's throat. The hare thrashed madly about trying to fling him off or to strike him with his clublike hind feet but the weasel, apparently limp now, hung on like death itself and within a minute the hare was down and struggling feebly. When I picked him up and kicked the weasel off with my boot he was dead, and the blood running from the wound left a scarlet stain on the white fur and the whiter snow.

Years later when I taught forest ecology at the University of Washington I lectured glibly about the "balance of nature" and often defended the predatory animals before my classes; but actually I have never been able to accept without question "the law of the tooth and the fang." To me it is not consistent with a "mother nature" concept to create animals who must prey upon brother animals. Since man can live healthfully on a vegetable diet, and the largest and most intelligent of the apes and the four-footed animals do so, I see no place for a normal predacity. I find evidence that this was not the planned state of nature in the fossil ancestors of the carnivores who were obviously herbaceous animals. So I feel sure that at some unhappy point in the long evolution of the cats, the dogs, and the weasels, some ancestor of these present carnivores, pressed no doubt by extreme hunger, took a wrong turn and made a wrong choice. To save his life he became a killer of his fellow creatures. To this extent, it seems to me, he retrogressed rather than evolved, although in most ways (the cats and dogs being among our more intelligent cousins) evolution continued upward.

No animal, of course, kills so much for his own pleasure and sustenance as man; and no other animal, except some of the ants, enslaves other animals (man calls it domestication) or, worse yet, breeds them by the millions to be slaughtered for food! And this in spite of the fact that we know we can get along well without meat. Man likewise must have made some wrong turns, although his progress has been generally upward. I am not a vegetarian myself, but I feel that I should be, and I am fully convinced that the growing of other intelligent animals as food is a barbarism which, like war, we will someday look back upon with shame.

13

THE FUNNY LITTLE CONY, OR ROCK RABBIT, piles up hay to cure on the rock slides during the summer, then stores it away in his "barns" under the huge stones for his winter's food supply. He then retires, like the good farmer that he is, to live with his family safe and snug through the long winter. He does not hibernate like the marmot or the bear, but is active and content within the walls of his house and barns.

So, as with the marmot and bear, we never saw them in winter, but some of the mantled ground squirrels and striped chipmunks came into the inn for their long sleep and we occasionally found one curled up in a dark corner dead to the world. The weasels knew this also and came into the hotel to hunt them. They also killed the mice and pack rats who remained active throughout the winter. I caught a tiny weasel one night in an ordinary spring mousetrap I had set in the pantry. He was no larger than my thumb, and he puzzled me as I skinned him out to save the skin for a specimen. I did not know any but the ordinary weasel, a foot or more in length, which I had trapped as a boy in Kansas. This midget was not white as other weasels were at this season, but the thing that puzzled me most was his half-pint dimensions. He was just about one good-sized mouse high but three mice long.

Later, when I became Park Naturalist to the National Park Service, I learned that there is a tribe of pygmy weasels, called "little" or "least" weasels, but at that time none of these had been reported from the Rainier area. I wrote the incident up in a small publication of nature notes which the Park Service put out and biologists immediately jumped on me, saying that I must be mistaken as I was way outside the recorded range of the "little" weasels. Unfortunately, I had by then mislaid my one specimen skin and I could not defend myself. However, it was only a year later that fieldmen of the Biological Survey did record the Streator little weasel inside the park and I was vindicated.

One very cold day in the middle of the winter I was prowling around and picked up a ball of brown fur in a dark upstairs linen room. I carried it in my pocket to our living room and laid it by the hot stove. It was a chipmunk and he appeared to be dead. I forgot him for a few minutes, but when I happened to look again he was sitting up scrubbing his face with his tiny paws. He was very much alive but obviously still a bit groggy from his sound sleep. I returned him, this time to the attic, where I suppose he promptly went back to sleep again. I hope that his dreams were not too violently interrupted and that he survived the winter in good shape.

14

IT BECAME A RITUAL EACH EVENING after supper to telephone Gus or Olga and chat with them about the weather or ourselves. Ruth exchanged recipes or housekeeping experiences with Olga, and often Gus had bits of news of the outside world which he heard over the radio or read in an occasional newspaper picked up at Ashford. Gus had a crystal set with earphones, but only occasionally when conditions were just right could he hear a Tacoma station. Without a radio or newspapers we contented ourselves mostly with allowing the rest of the world to take care of itself and do its own worrying. As for us, we were no longer part of the ordinary world; we lived far above it in a special paradise of our own.

Our living room was the employees' dining room during the summer, and the hotel bakeshop had been temporarily converted into a kitchen for our winter use. Our bedroom was the chef's private room, and the hotel pantry had been stocked with a truckload of food to carry us through till spring. Each day we took a market basket in one hand and a lantern in the other and went shopping at our private supermarket. There was a great variety of tinned meats, fruits, and vegetables to choose from and there were no price tags. Gus bought fresh meat, fruits, and vegetables, when available, for us at Ashford. These I packed up almost weekly when I went down for our mail.

In the cavern-like dining room of the hotel I found a huge supply of cedar logs and a sharp saw. These had been dragged in early the previous fall when the hotel closed for the season, and stacked on planks laid on the main dining room floor. The wood would warm me once as I cut and split it in the dining room and again as I wheeled it through the hotel kitchen into our living room and we burned it in the big airtight stove placed there.

Since we had the entire hotel to draw upon, our private quarters in the bakeshop and the help's dining room were very well furnished indeed. Ruth made them bright and attractive with rugs, cushions, and curtains. What we lacked in light we tried to compensate for with color. The best light we had was from Coleman lanterns, but there was an ample supply of candles in the storeroom and we used them lavishly. It was really quite cozy on long winter evenings, and I do not remember that we missed the outside world very much. Part of this contentment came from physical well-being, part from our love of each other and dreams of a family of our own already in prospect; but partially too it was due, I think, to a reaction from the years of war and separation. We were at last together—and wishful thinking, plus ignorance of the real state of health throughout the world, led us to think that this war had really ended all wars and that peace was assured throughout our time. How wrong we were! After a second, vastly more disastrous world catastrophe, we have still not learned that peace cannot be had by fighting wars, nor have we learned how to build a brotherhood among mankind based on justice and equality.

15

RUTH'S GREATEST DOMESTIC PROBLEMS faced her in the bakeshop which was our kitchen and dining room. It was equipped to serve hundreds of people and we were only two. Everything was to scale except us. One of the smaller ranges had been moved in from the hotel kitchen, but it was so huge that when we stoked it enough to bake in its cavernous oven it made the entire room so hot we had to open all the windows. It was a coal-burning range, but we burned wood in it, starting the fires with kerosene. This was standard procedure on the Kansas farm where I grew up. Father always kept a box of clean corncobs beside the stove and a can of kerosene—often with a small potato stuck on the spout because the cap had been mislaid. We filled the firebox with cobs, dashed kerosene over them, and threw in a lighted match. Instantly we had a roaring fire. In France we had often started cooking fires by placing a few sticks of high-explosive powder, which we took from shell cases, under our kindling. The result in either case was entirely successful so far as getting a hot fire quickly was concerned. I used the same method in our kitchen at Paradise.

There are, of course, certain precautions that must be taken if this form of incendiarism is to be reasonably safe. The stove should be cold, you should be ready to cover the flames quickly, and you should be sure that it goes off the first time you try. Ruth was not as experienced in this ritual as I was and one day she nearly blew the place up.

There were, unknown to her, some live coals left in the ashes of the night before and she was not as quick with her match as she should have been. Inflammable gas had formed in the stove and in the room, and when she struck her match the whole place exploded in her face. I rushed in to find the room full of smoke and soot, Ruth as black as the stove and her eyebrows completely burned away. She, understandably, refused to start the fires after that.

16

NOT ALL WAS SUNSHINE IN PARADISE.

There were weeks at a time when neither the sun nor the moon could break through the clouds and the snow fell like eiderdown in great fluffy masses. It was no use to dig out our light tunnels then, for they filled right up again, so we sat by our gasoline lanterns and read and listened to the phonograph. Fortunately there was plenty of music. Ruth had discovered the hotel's piano the first day and we promptly moved it into our quarters. Almost every evening she played and sang. To her it was a real tie with the world she had known so well. There were times, when the mood was on her, when she attacked the piano with a rage that sent Brahms sonatas roaring through the echoing building and must even have disturbed the chipmunks sleeping out their winter nights.

Although Ruth practiced the piano for several hours on most days, she still had time to sew and cook. She learned by hard experience that it takes hours longer to boil beans or rice at high altitudes than it does at sea level, and that baking powders and yeasts do not function in the same way. There are recipe books available now for high-altitude cookery, but she had to learn by trial and error. (We ate most of the errors but some of them were strictly for the birds.)

Boiled foods take more time because water boils at a lower temperature than it does at sea level. I remember that Hans Fuhrer, our tough Swiss head guide, used to astonish amateur climbers by drinking boiling tea at Camp Muir. (At ten thousand feet elevation water boils at 190° Fahrenheit.) A pressure cooker would have solved this problem for us, but we had no such modern device.

Why cakes fell flat and bread would not rise at all, we never knew. Ruth finally learned that you must use more flour and less baking powder and beat eggs less as well as bake everything more slowly. She mastered the art of alpine cookery to such a degree that once with one huge meal, served to twenty-five or thirty men of the early crew (who had hiked in over the trail on July first to ready the hotel for the Fourth of July opening), she established a reputation as a cook which they still refer to after all these years.

Gray jays

They say it is the lemon meringue pie that shines brightest in their memories, but Ruth thinks it was the long hike they had had up from Narada Falls that really seasoned the dishes.

Next to the outside wall of our kitchen there were electric baking ovens reaching to head height for summer use. These we used for storage space—they were mouse-tight. There were huge mixing tables along the rest of the wall. Our stove was near the far end. The remainder of the room we used for our dining area.

Naturally, the pots and pans were on the same scale as the stoves and ovens. Ruth mixed cakes for two in mixing bowls large enough for baby baths and fried two eggs on Paul Bunyan griddles.

Actually we seldom cooked for two only, because there were always our bird neighbors. The bakeshop was situated in a wing on the downhill side so the end windows were actually third-floor windows. The tops of those were never quite covered with snow and outside one of them we kept a bird-feeding platform. A half dozen Clark's crows and numerous gray jays, juncos, and rosy finches became our closest neighbors and most intimate companions. No morning passed, except during the most violent storms, that some of them were not on hand waiting in our bread line.

Most of these clients were patient, even shy, but the crows and jays are not long on such virtues as patience and demureness. If we slept late and were tardy with the bacon and toast, the crows would rap sharply on the windowpane with their heavy beaks, and then cock a baleful eye at us. I really think they thought that they owned the place and we were their servants.

I often amused myself by playing tricks on them. Since the crows seldom ate their food at the shelf but carried it away to a nearby hemlock where they could eat in greater privacy or store the food with the other supplies they kept there, I would sometimes nail the food down to the shelf or tie it with strings to torment them. A sadistic variation of this minor torture was to tie a piece of food with a long string so that when the crow or jay flew away with it the string would snatch it back, causing them to tumble over in mid-air, or to ground-loop if they were flying too low. Sometimes I would put out stale biscuits too hard to be broken and so heavy that they could hardly fly with them. It was amusing to see them stagger through the air as overburdened as drunken sailors.

This, of course, amused no one but me and did not discourage our feathered friends. Later in the winter both the gray jays and the Clark's crows became so bold that they would take food from our hand, and on several occasions when the window was left open they came into the house to pilfer. One day a crow tried to take meat from a frying pan on the hot stove but changed his mind when he burned his feet. A gray jay actually tried to fly away with a quarter-pound of butter from the table as we were eating our dinner. It was heavier and more slippery than he had figured so he never got airborne with it, but he made a very good try. This is why these saucy jays are sometimes called "camp robbers" in the Northwest.

17

APPARENTLY ALL I HAD TO DO to hold down this heavenly job was to keep a daily record for the Weather Bureau's Seattle office and report by telephone about once a week to the company office in Tacoma. This I usually did through Gus at Longmire. For this I received a fair monthly wage. Our food was free—truckloads of all sorts of food ready on the shelf—and Ruth was even being paid to cook it for us. There was an enormous roof over our heads, fuel in our bins, water at the tap; we had comfort and security—all kinds of security, and we were sure we would live happily together all the rest of our lives. In the evening when the sunset glow climbed quickly up the ice dome of the mountain and was reflected across Paradise Valley, the pearly gates stood wide-open and all our streets were really paved with gold.

Later it developed that there were other chores to be done. There were dormer windows to be shored up and rescued from the shifting mass of snow on the roof, tunnels to be opened and extended each time it snowed, garbage to be hauled out on a toboggan and buried deep in a pit under the snow, and furniture to be built and repaired in the shop. Then there were the weekly trips to Longmire for mail and fresh supplies, and eventually a long tunnel to be dug to the coal bins when the wood supply began to give out.

All these things we enjoyed doing. On mild days we explored the valley on skis and I practiced jumping on a small take-off which I built on the hill back of the hotel. When I became more sure of myself on skis I used them for the trip down to Longmire, carrying webs on my back for the long uphill climb home. Once I made the trip down in forty minutes, but before I got that good I had knocked the bark off of a good many trees along the trail—and considerable bark off myself as well. One time I skied into the Paradise River and came close to losing my life. A hole had opened in one of the many crossings which I did not see in time to stop. I fell ten feet or more into the icy water, breaking my skis. Fortunately, the water was shallow and I was able, by using a part of the broken ski, to dig myself out. I had lost my pack, I was bruised and breathless and I was wet, but fortunately I was near Narada Falls so I built a fire in the cabin there, and dried out my clothing. Otherwise I might have frozen.

I usually left the skis at Longmire and climbed back up the hill on snowshoes with our supplies on my back. When spring came they had to send a truck down to National Park Inn for the pile of skis that had accumulated there.

The trip back up took four or five hours, and even longer if there was new snow. I never set out in bad weather, but once I was caught in an unexpected blizzard and found myself in real trouble. I wore a squirrel-skin parka which kept me warm, but I had no goggles and the hard snow blew into my hood and cut my face. At times I could hardly see and had to feel my way along the trail. Fortunately by then I knew the terrain well and I had been over the trail so many times that even with the drifting new snow there was usually a trough where the trail should be.

I barely made it to Narada cabin that day but the telephone worked so I was able to call Ruth and Gus and allay their mounting fears. I spent the afternoon at Narada and by evening the wind had slackened and the snow abated enough so that I could go on into Paradise before dark.

Really big storms usually gave us some advance warning. High clouds or dull skies changed the entire aspect of the valley. The snow so brilliant in sunlight became gray and flat. It was difficult, and even dangerous, to ski or snowshoe on such days. Small depressions and irregularities in the surface were totally invisible because of the lack of revealing shadows. Many times I fell down steep hills or into deep troughs in the snow because I could not see them directly in front of me.

I made it a habit to go out and look up at the mountain each evening before darkness set in. This seemed more reliable than a falling barometer. If the peak was entirely covered with clouds my weather gauge was hidden and I could not tell. It might mean the coming of a storm but more often they were local clouds which would drift away again. But if the snow dome, which seemed so close on sunny days that you could all but reach out and touch it, was distant and gray, we prepared for snow. If long streamers of snow were driven from the summit there would likely be wind also and heavy drifting in the meadows.

In heavy winds and snow we did not dare go outside the inn. Fifty feet from the tunnel mouth was too far. There were no landmarks then except the slope of the ground and even that might mislead you for where the ground sloped down today it might slope upward tomorrow because of shifting drifts. A high wind could literally blow you away, to become exhausted and covered with snow before you could fight your way back. No one would find you until the spring thaw. Such an accident occurred during the past winter. A skier left his party in a fog at Panorama Point to run directly back to the inn while the others went on around the rim of Edith Creek Basin. He did not arrive at the inn and days of search failed to find him. When the snow melts in July he may be found but if he veered too far to the right and was lost on the Nisqually Glacier, his body may be swallowed up by the crevasses and never found.

18

LUCKILY RUTH AND I FOUND NO DIFFICULTY in employing our time creatively, and the most creative thing we did that year, by all odds, was to start a family. By January Ruth suspected that she was pregnant and by February she was certain. She began making baby clothing and I spent many equally happy hours in the carpenter's shop building the baby a bed. Since there is nothing so old-fashioned as having a baby, I, with no concern for functionalism, decided to make our child an old-fashioned cradle (it was only good fortune that I did not decide to build it an Indian cradle board). I remembered a picture in an old history book of the cradle built in Roanoke for little Virginia Dare and I modeled our cradle after that one. It was, you remember, the sort with a wooden hood at the head, but which from the foot looked more like a tiny casket on rockers than a bed.

However, it turned out nicely and after I had polished the yellow cedar boards smoothly and Ruth had lined it with a pink silk, hand-quilted pad and put a fringe of lace around the hood, it was very pretty and we hid it away to await the big event. Our son, who arrived late the next September, still has it, and each of his four children have used it in their turn.

I always enjoy working with wood and we had a huge supply of the finest wood I have ever worked with in our firewood supply of Alaska cedar logs in the hotel dining room.

About two miles down the ski trail on a small flat below Narada Falls there was a forest of "ghost" trees, called the Silver Forest. For some reason there had been an almost pure stand of Alaska yellow cedar growing there. Then, when the largest trees were about two feet in diameter and fifty feet tall, they were all killed by a fire. At this elevation trees grow slowly so these were very old, and the wood of a very fine texture. New undergrowth indicated that the trees had been killed thirty or forty years before and during these years the winter storms, aided by insects, had stripped them of all bark and most branches, and the summer suns had bleached the surface of the logs to a lovely silver gray. The wood, being decay resistant as all cedars are, had only become harder and darker in color. Now it worked smoothly and finished a rich satin yellow. It also has a pleasant, pungent odor which I never smell without remembering the hours I spent ankle-deep in cedar shavings in the carpenter shop under Paradise Inn. The only other wood I know which is as satisfying to work is the hinoki cedar so admired by Japanese craftsmen. The two species are closely related botanically.

I built not only the cradle that winter but numerous yellow cedar candlesticks, book ends, hand-carved toys, and pieces of furniture. Most of them we gave to our friends later but some we still have. Just the other day I met an old lady, now blind, whom I had not seen for twenty-five years and whom I had forgotten entirely. The first thing she told me was that she still has and uses an alpenstock I had made and given to her when she visited the valley many years ago.

I also enjoyed the long hours I spent sawing firewood from the pile of yellow cedar logs in the hotel dining room. A gasoline pressure lantern lighted up the place well enough to work and cast eerie shadows into the far corners of the room; shadows which pumped steadily up and down until a block of firewood fell, and then dashed madly about the walls and ceiling as I swung an ax to split the block into pieces. Soon the pile of yellow sawdust was ankle-deep and the pleasant odor of Alaska cedar spread throughout the entire building.

When I had finished cutting and splitting a day's supply of wood I wheeled it into the back hall and stacked it there. From this pile we carried what we needed into the bakeshop where we cooked our meals, and upstairs for our living room stove. It took a lot of wood to keep both fires going—even for honeymooners.

On many of these silver-gray logs I found fascinating designs etched deep into the wood. These, I knew, were made by a species of bark beetle when the trees had first died many years ago. The brush fire which had killed the trees had not burned them. Bark beetles had nested under the bark and their young had fed on the rich cambium layer between the outer bark and the hard wood. Tiny wormlike bark beetle larvae had created these strange designs. I saved some of the most beautiful by cutting the blocks into book ends, candlesticks, and other useful objects with the insect engravings to provide a decorative touch.

I had studied forest entomology in college so I could read the fascinating story of the life cycle of these tiny beetles who engrave in wood. It is easy to see where the brown-colored, round-ended female beetle, who in this species is about one-eighth of an inch long and half that in diameter, entered through the bark of the injured tree and began to carve out a snug nest cavity for herself with her strong jaws. She did not eat the wood as termites do, but pushed it out the tiny entrance hole where it collected on the bark or at the foot of the tree. It was this sign perhaps which guided the male beetle to where she waited for him to fertilize her eggs. The story of this romantic encounter was not told in the wood but the results of it very quickly became apparent, for the mother beetle, in a flurry of energy, began immediately to extend the nuptial cavity into a brood chamber leading in a straight line for about two inches up the trunk of the tree. As she worked, never stopping to rest or to feed, she deposited eggs and packed each in the frass from her busy jaws. At the end of her tunnel (and her egg-laying) she died. These large straight nest cavities were the backbone of the designs I found.

Now the tiny eggs began to hatch one after the other in quick succession, and the hard-headed and voracious little grubs began to eat their way into adulthood. As each took off alternately to the right and the left, they left a hair-line tunnel behind them, but as the grub grew in size the tunnels widened to accommodate him, and as they widened they had to expand and flare out. This brought about the butterfly designs I admired. By the time the grub had gnawed and digested his way for about three inches his tunnel was as large as that of the brood tunnel from which he had branched off as a baby beetle.

Here for the first time in his life, he paused and began to go through that miraculous metamorphosis which changes a worm-like grub into an adult insect as different from its juvenile form as a swan is from a crocodile, although technically it is the same species of "bug."

As soon as the young adult bark beetle emerged from the chrysalis stage at the end of his tunnel, he was ready and eager to gnaw his way out through the bark, leaving a tiny exit hole only a few inches removed in distance, but a generation removed in time, from the hole where his mother had entered on her honeymoon. I wondered if the young beetles faced the new world with as much energy and enthusiasm as their mother had apparently faced her destiny. The new brood of fifty or sixty boy and girl beetles then flew away to other trees to complete the life cycle of the bark beetles.

Unfortunately, there were tragic endings to this otherwise happy little domestic tale which I read in my woodpile. One such ending was accidental. Young bark beetles apparently do not have an unerring sense of direction, and evidence engraved in the hard wood showed that many of them turned inward, rather than outward, when they were ready to emerge. Apparently these never discovered their mistake but wore their lives out in a frantic effort to find the other side of the tree—a sad turn of events for young knights and ladies who otherwise would be out pursuing or being pursued by their mates.

The other tragedy was not an accident to the beetle but to the host, the tree. Bark beetles often infest healthy trees and if enough colonies are formed on the same tree some of the tunnels are sure to overlap until the tree is completely girdled and the upward movement of the life-giving sap is completely cut off. Such trees eventually die of strangulation and starvation. Millions of board feet of commercial timber are destroyed every year in this manner. In most Western states where raging forest fires annually destroy thousands of acres of valuable standing timber and do millions of dollars' worth of additional damage to wildlife, ground cover, and private property, the inconspicuous little bark beetles do even greater damage than the fires and they are much harder to control. In the Silver Forest, where the trees would have died anyway from the fire, the two enemies of the forest had cooperated.

19

AS THE WOOD SUPPLY DIMINISHED in the dining room and the winter weather dragged on we began to be worried, wondering if our fuel would last until spring. There was ample standing timber near the hotel but park rules forbade our cutting any trees for any purpose, so on one of my weekly reports to the Tacoma office I mentioned our problem and asked for advice. I was told not to worry, "If the wood runs out there is a big pile of coal just outside the kitchen door."

The wood was short enough already so I felt it would be wise to verify this bit of information. But that, I found, was not easy to do. The back kitchen door was on the uphill side of the kitchen wing and there was still some twenty feet of hard-packed snow piled against it. Besides this the door opened out—or would open out if the snow were removed. I started digging but packed snow is harder to move than hard soil and I soon decided that it would be easier to replace the door than to move the snow. So I broke the door down.

All I could see through the opening was snow, but somewhere out there to the right or the left—or perhaps straight ahead—was coal. All I had to do was find and mine it. I got an ax and a shovel and started hacking away at the ice-hard wall and very soon I had the problem of what to do with my "mine dump." We couldn't have the kitchen full of snow! The only thing I could see to do with it was throw it out a window. That was possible because the inn is built on a steep hillside, and while all the upper side of the kitchen wing is at ground level the other side is one floor above ground level and the far end of the bakeshop, which is a wing off the kitchen wing, is three floors aboveground. Here on the canyon side of the building the snow had by now settled until it was below the level of the third-floor windows.

I got the wheelbarrow and started wheeling away the pile which had already accumulated inside the kitchen door. This meant a long back-stretch between the work tables and the three kitchen ranges, a sharp right turn between the ranges and the pantry beyond, a left through the door into the back hall, a dog-leg right to hit the door into the bakeshop, and finally a straightaway down the home stretch between the mixing tables and our kitchen range. Now all I had to do was open the bakeshop window, shovel the snow out, and get it closed again before Ruth began to feel the draft.

Still this did not seem too difficult since I had, or thought that I had, plenty of time. But this digging and wheeling went on for days and days and every day as the tunnels got longer the woodpile got smaller. Actually I never did strike coal.

We began to ration the wood, the weather turned warmer, and we made out, but only after we had burned all the sawdust and chips and the planking on which the logs had been piled.

After all the snow had melted, which was near the end of July, I went back and looked to see where the coal had been keeping itself. It was there all right, but not "just outside" the kitchen door. My first lateral to the right had gone about ten feet and missed it by a foot. The others had been nowhere near it.

20

Snowed in by late winter storms, and just for fun, Ruth and I designed a houseful of pine-cone "birds." Near the mineral springs at Longmire there are a few gnarled old lodgepole pines. Lodgepole (*Pinus contorta*) gets its species name from its small lopsided cone. I picked a pocketful of these queer little cones one day when I was down for mail, and took them home with me. With a saucy head, carved from wood and painted in bright colors, glued to the stem end of the cone, and a big flat foot to stand on, a swell-chested cocky little bird evolved. We christened him "Dippy Duck."

Before the winter was over we had the top of the piano almost covered with a whole flock of Dippy Ducks, Woody Woodpeckers, Henry Herons, Peter Pelicans, Sammy Storks, Oscar Owls, and other strange and sundry species. On some I put tiny skis or snowshoes and these Nordic "he-birds" sported bright mufflers and flowing stocking caps which Ruth knit for them, as well as such names as Lars the Lark, and Sven the Swan. For each bird I hand-labeled a tiny calling card and we had a lot of fun hatching a new name for each new creation.

Dippy Duck

When we made them we had no idea of selling them but they so pleased the manager of the hotel gift shop when she saw them later in the spring that she begged to buy them. Some of the more pretentious of our flock sold that summer for as much as five dollars each, and I went back to the College of Forestry in the fall in a fine new serge suit paid for with a pocketful of pine cones. Not inappropriate, I thought, that the forest should help pay for the training of its foresters.

21

MR. MARTIN HAD TOLD US THAT WE might not see another human being until late spring, when the maintenance crews would come in to ready the hotel for the coming season. However, if the telephone line should go out government linemen would come up to repair it, and if the trouble was high up in the valley they might come on to spend a night with us at the inn. Forest telephone lines are strung loosely through open insulators so that if a heavy branch or a snag falls on the line during a storm there is enough slack and the line, even if borne down to the ground, usually does not break. Our prospects of having visitors seemed slight.

So we were surprised one day when Gus called about noon and asked if we had a visitor. According to Gus a young lawyer from Chicago named Wilson had shown up unannounced at Longmire Springs and planned to stay on for a few days. He had said he was on vacation for his health. It seems he had some incurable disease and the doctors had advised him to take things easy. He decided he might as well live it up a bit while he still had time and started out immediately to see those parts of the world which lie beyond Cook County.

The evening before, he had asked about Paradise Valley and mentioned that he would like to hike up there. They told him the trail was not open and thought no more about it, but in the morning after breakfast he had left the inn and he hadn't come back. Gus had just gone out and followed his trail for a mile—he was headed for Paradise Valley. He was dressed in ordinary street clothes and shoes, so Gus was worried. Fortunately, it was a mild, clear day.

I told Gus that I would look around and call him back. I immediately put on my skis and ran down the trail as far as Narada Falls. There was no sign of our man anywhere along the way. When I got back about two I called Gus again. Wilson had not returned there. I waited an hour and called again. No word yet.

So Gus notified the park rangers and I started back down the trail. This time I carried an extra pair of snowshoes, and some hot coffee and sandwiches.

I found him sitting in the snow by the ski trail in a steep chute we called the Devil's Dip. He was very tired and his feet were wet and cold, but otherwise he seemed in very good shape for a sick man so far from home. I left a note for the rangers at Narada cabin, and we started up the hill. With the food and coffee inside him, and with snowshoes on his feet we got along fairly well, but it was well after dark and Mr. Wilson was exhausted when we finally reached the inn.

I had called Ruth from Narada, and she had a good dinner waiting for us. As soon as he got into dry socks and my fur-lined house slippers he was ready to eat. He seemed excited and happy about the adventure; it apparently had not entered his head that if Gus had not missed him, and if I had not found him before dark, he would surely have frozen back there in the Devil's Dip.

During dinner we were telling him of our life in Paradise Valley, and of the good times we had had skiing and tobogganing. He said that he would like to tackle the toboggan run. It was about nine by the time dinner was over and the things cleared away, but there was a full moon and the mountain was clear and bright in the greenish light. It was so bright I remember that the trees cast blue-black shadows on the snow.

So we put on heavy clothing, took the toboggan, and went up the hill.

Thinking back on that experience we know now that we made three serious errors in judgment. First, to give the guy his money's worth, we went about fifty yards farther up the hill than usual. Second, there was a hundred and fifty pounds more weight on the sled than we had ever carried before. And third, it was late and cold, and a crust had formed on the track.

We did not consider these important factors at the moment. Ruth and I had made the run safely many times before, and we were quite willing to display our skill. Ruth got on first, belly flop (which is the only safe way to ride a toboggan downhill), Wilson was next, and I shoved off from the rear where I could steer and brake a little with my feet.

We took off fast, and just as soon as we were under way I knew that we were headed for trouble.

At the bottom of the hill there was a narrow snow valley and then a sharp, steep rise some thirty feet high. Actually, this was a big drift covering the two-story employees' dormitory, although at that time we did not know what was underneath the snow. For us it had been a good stopping place. We usually ran about halfway up the rise and then slowed to a gentle stop.

This night I think we were doing at least a hundred miles an hour. At the bottom of the hill we crossed the little valley and shot up the rise beyond. We didn't even hesitate at the top but went sailing on free into the air. A moment later we landed in a heap and lay there. Ruth and I knew that there was a five-hundred-foot drop into the canyon just beyond. Wilson was the first to get up and brush himself off. He was bleeding from the nose but unaware of it yet. He was excited and happy as a kid. "That was fun!" he yelled. "Let's go up and do it again."

I was shaking like a monkey in a blizzard and I thought my wrist was broken. Ruth had skinned the side of her face and torn one ear. We left the toboggan buried in the snow and went back to the inn—we had put on too good a show for us, if not for our guest.

When we had cleaned up and drunk a cup of hot coffee, Wilson was ready to turn in. It had been a big day for us all.

Early next morning I sneaked out and looked at our track. At the foot of the hill we had left the ground entirely for about twenty feet and at the top we had jumped more than thirty feet, landing less than a hundred feet from the rim of the canyon.

I took Mr. Wilson down to Longmire the next day and Ruth and I decided that for an invalid he had done pretty well. We predicted that his next trip to "Paradise" might be longer delayed than his doctors had believed.

22

NOT EVERY DAY IN PARADISE WAS A DREAM. Some of our most violent storms came in March. Living under a mountainous snowdrift we could not hear the wind. The huge wooden building would creak and groan every night as the snow settled and bore down upon it, but not having a radio we heard no weather predictions. We learned to be our own weather prophets.

It often happened that our first evidence of a storm outside was to wake up at eight o'clock in the morning in midnight darkness. The tunnels had all been snowed over or drifted full in the night. On such occasions the first chore after breakfast was to shovel our way out. If there was a full-blown storm in progress there was little use to do this as the tunnel would fill up again as fast as we opened it. So for days at a time, during February and March, and once or twice in April, we were snowbound, totally and completely.

Paradise Valley lies between five and seven thousand feet elevation. This is not high country in the Rockies; Denver is about the same elevation; but on the west slope of the Cascades it is high. Timberline on Mount Rainier is around seven thousand feet and the heaviest snows, sometimes more than one hundred feet a year, fall below that elevation. There is never one hundred feet of snow on the ground at any one time, except in canyons, but I measured that total at the weather gauge. Some melts or evaporates even in winter and the rest gradually settles and packs until there is seldom more than thirty feet on the level. But this snow by spring is so hard-packed that it will hold horses easily and even the heavy power shovels and bulldozers which are used by the Park Service to open the roads in the early summer. That year the steam shovel got through to the inn on the Fourth of July. It is later some years.

23

AS THE LONG WINTER STRETCHED OUT into what the calendar on the wall boldly insisted was spring, it began to appear as if spring, if it came at all, might pass in the night and so completely elude us. We became very sensitive to any sign of the season and at times talked about little else than the coming of spring. One of the strangest of these signs appeared quite suddenly in late June as blood-red patches in the melting snow. The first place we noticed looked as if some pre-season picnickers had been feasting on watermelon. Although it was an exciting discovery it did not mystify me, as I had read of this tiny yeastlike plant, a protococcus algae, which often grows in old snow at this latitude. However, for a time, I kept my superior knowledge to myself and tried to confuse Ruth with tales of bloody encounters between mythical mountain characters who according to Indian legends roam the glaciers and snowfields on dark and stormy nights. One of the best-known of these truculent mountain spirits, named Enumclaw, was said to live in the crater at the summit of the mountain from where he hurled stones at his estranged brother, Kapoonis, who dwelt in the crater of Mount Hood a hundred miles to the south. Kapoonis returned stone for stone and it was the clash of these missiles overhead that caused thunder and lightning. In the exuberance of spring they may come down upon the snowfields and do battle hand to hand, leaving their bloody mark upon the snow. Although she did not fall for my stories she was much mystified, as newcomers to the mountain often are, by this strange phenomenon.

Actually the fact is almost as difficult to believe as the fiction, for the algae are primitive, microscopic plants which grow normally and happily in the snow. They are related to the green algae, often called "moss," which grow like dabs of powdery green paint on the shady side of trees (for the express purpose, I am told, of informing Boy Scouts lost in the woods which direction is north). Other green algae form scum on stagnant water and some contract an "interracial" marriage with certain fungus plants and together form the fascinating plant we call a lichen. All are protococci and most are green, but these are blood-red. Under the microscope the tiny one-celled plants look like clusters of toy balloons. Yeastlike they grow rapidly under favorable conditions at the surface of the melting snow, expand, divide into two daughter cells, and so, multiplying by geometric ratio, spread into broad crimson patches on the snowfields. When the snow has all melted and run away, the tiny balloons shrivel up and lie dormant on the ground throughout the summer and the following winter. How the revitalized parent cells get back to the hard surface through ten or fifteen feet of compact snow in order to vegetate and reproduce again during the brief spring thaw I do not know.

When snow ceased to fall so often and the old snow packed so hard in the trail that I didn't need snowshoes for the climb back up, the weekly trip to Longmire was a joy. I could swoop down the trail early in the morning on skis and be back in Paradise by noon. Spring came six weeks earlier at Longmire than at Paradise Valley, and there were always new things to discover along the trail. These discoveries I reported to Ruth upon my return, and occasionally Gus or Mr. Martin would send up a special treat for her, such as bananas or a head of lettuce. And, although the picking of flowers is strictly forbidden by park regulations, I sometimes took her flaming bouquets of red currant, and once a lady's slipper orchid which bloomed in May in the lower woods when we were still deep under snow in Paradise Valley.

Another sure sign of spring was the magpies. These large black-and-white cousins-of-a-crow live typically in the dry areas of the Western plains and the Great Basin, where they build their grotesque castles of rough sticks and other rubbish in the cottonwoods and willows beside the occasional rivers and smaller streams. But each year a few hardy adventurous individuals cross over the high summits of the Cascades and come into the upper valleys of Mount Rainier. It is the season for nesting and all conventional magpie families are busily engaged in this domestic enterprise on their home ranges, but these few *voyageurs* apparently do not nest. It may be that they are jilted males or bachelor magpies, who turn explorer for a season and take up mountaineering to escape boredom. Anyway, by the middle of June stray magpies, like evil spirits, were dropping from tree to tree in Paradise Valley and casting sidelong looks at our feeding shelf. But they never ventured so close as to partake of the free lunch we provided, whether from fear of us or of their cousins, once removed, the Clark's crows.

Soon after this we had the first vocal announcements of the approach of spring. They came from the air, but not by radio. Spring was heralded by all the songbirds singing. The sooty grouse, although by no stretch of the imagination a songbird, was first to boom out the good news.

The author and his wife Ruth soon after they came to Mount Rainier National Park. (Photo by Floyd Schmoe)

There are many grouse in the high meadows, where they spend a lonely winter huddled among the dense branches of the alpine firs and hemlocks. Occasionally we had seen their chicken-like tracks in the snow but I do not remember having seen or heard one all winter.

Then one morning (it must already have been June) there were "hooters" on every hill, even though there was yet ten feet of snow on the ground and it was still winter to us. It did not look like—it only sounded like—spring.

The hooting of the sooty grouse when in love is beyond description in mere words. It *belongs* to the high country and would be out of place in any setting less alpine. It is a muffled *whoo, whoo, whoo,* that goes on at intervals for hours on end. It sounds like something pumped out of a bellows by a ventriloquist, and that is in fact just what it is. It is difficult to locate the hooter because he sounds far away when he is very near, and near when he is far away.

We went out looking for him one morning and finally, down by the garbage dump, we located our harbinger of spring. He was perched on a matted branch forty feet up in a hemlock tree, and although he saw us watching him he went right on about his business undisturbed. To him it was the most important business in the world, for he was hooting up a mate. As we watched he squatted on the branch, spread his tail feathers, and drooped his wings far down and backward. Then he blew up the bright yellow pouches on either side of his neck until he looked like a new football. Now, with a rhythmic pumping motion of his head, he let out the weird, evenly timed hoots until he was deflated again. All this time he was fluttering his drooping wings, adding a visual tremolo to his "song." I never saw a lovesick crooner who put more umph into his performance. There was no female grouse in sight but I'm sure many were within sound range, and if it was a thrilling sound to us hootless mortals, what must it have been to a broody hen grouse?

The gray jays and the Clark's crows were nesting around Narada Falls and those of Paradise Valley were obviously thinking about it. There were more visible signs of spring also, which I saw a few days later when skiing along timberline ridge. The ptarmigan were out and there was gray among the pure white feathers of their winter plumage. The molt had begun, and soon they would be gray and white to blend with the rocks of the glacier rim, as their white coats had blended all winter with the snow. And down in the valleys the snowshoe rabbits and the ermine, in anticipation of the coming season, had already changed to their brown summer coats.

Certainly spring, if not already here, was coming up very fast.

spring

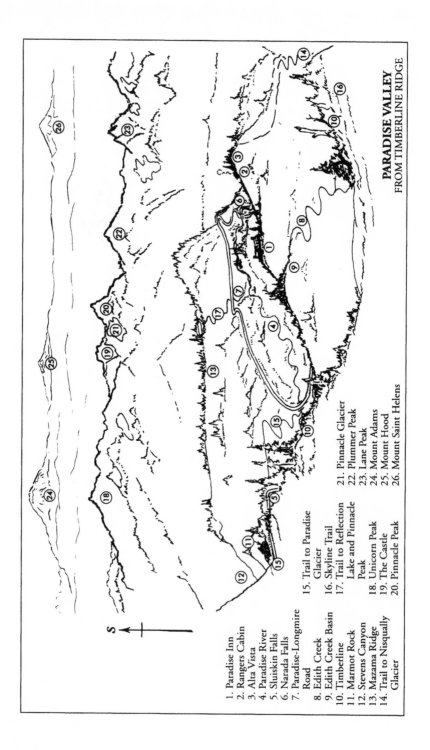

1. Paradise Inn
2. Rangers Cabin
3. Alta Vista
4. Paradise River
5. Sluiskin Falls
6. Narada Falls
7. Paradise-Longmire Road
8. Edith Creek
9. Edith Creek Basin
10. Timberline
11. Marmot Rock
12. Stevens Canyon
13. Mazama Ridge
14. Trail to Nisqually Glacier
15. Trail to Paradise Glacier
16. Skyline Trail
17. Trail to Reflection Lake and Pinnacle Peak
18. Unicorn Peak
19. The Castle
20. Pinnacle Peak
21. Pinnacle Glacier
22. Plummer Peak
23. Lane Peak
24. Mount Adams
25. Mount Hood
26. Mount Saint Helens

PARADISE VALLEY
FROM TIMBERLINE RIDGE

1

SPRING COMES SUDDENLY IN PARADISE Valley and it passes quickly. But there *is* spring, and it is the most exciting season of all the year. Whereas winter sleeps in peace and beauty on the face of the mountain, spring brings joyful awakening.

Everything happens at once. Everything is in a hurry. The snow can't wait to melt; the water can't wait to rush down the swollen rivers. The flowers can't wait to blossom and mature their precious seed; the birds can't wait to nest and rear their young; and the tourists can't wait to get on the mountain. (That spring we could hardly wait to get off the mountain.) Everyone knows that the snows and winter's sleep will come again too soon.

It was late in June that first year before the seductive breath of spring really engulfed the valley. I noticed it before I got out of bed one morning, having been awakened early by an agonized groaning and creaking of the roof over our heads. All winter the huge frame building had been protesting the terrific burden of snow it was forced to carry, and we had often wondered why it did not collapse completely. It is for this reason that the roof of Paradise Inn is pitched very steeply, like a letter A, so that the snow, although it cannot slide off (for the simple reason that there is no place for so much snow to go), does sit astride the building resting largely upon the ground on either side and not upon the structure itself. Still, as it settles and solidifies, it grips its victim in a deadly squeeze, and each winter extensive damage is done to the roof which must be repaired by the maintenance crews each spring. More than once entire dormer windows have been torn away by the settling snow.

This morning I heard its rending crunch. The beams over our heads were moaning as though they were being twisted by a giant's hands. As wakefulness gradually cleared the sleepy mists from my mind I began to

Ice-coated alpine fir trees in Paradise Valley after an early spring thaw. (Photo by Questa from Linsley)

notice that the air that blew in through the open window was not sharp and cold as it usually was in the early morning hours, but soft and balmy like a gentle caress. So instead of slipping out from between the warm covers, closing the window quickly and jumping back into bed again, as I more often did, I breathed in a deep draft of the warm air and called to Ruth to get up and enjoy the spring. The chinook had come!

This chinook wind is one of the famous winds of the world and one of the joys of the Pacific Northwest. Unlike the mistral of Europe, which blows cold, and the simoon of Arabia, which blows hot and dry, the chinook brings warm moist air off the Pacific Ocean onto the Northwest coast. It performs miracles. Under its magic touch Indian maidens burst into songs of love and longing; king salmon madly charge high waterfalls and actually swim straight up through the falling water; birds "bust" out all over and fill the countryside with song; and winter melts away with the dispatch of the proverbial snowball in hell. We dressed hurriedly and went outside. We breathed in great gasps of the tropic air and wallowed in its embraces. Even the snow felt warmer to the touch and in an exuberance of gaiety I took a big handful of the crystal stuff and washed Ruth's face. At that she grabbed a ski pole and chased me around the inn.

We had a late breakfast and started out on a long hike of exploration. For some time now the snow had been so hard that we did not need snow-shoes or skis. Down on the flat below the inn what had been domes of snow were overnight the gables and ridgepoles of undiscovered buildings. There were stables, dormitories, a laundry, campground store, comfort stations, and shelters, of whose existence we had never known. We poked into gable windows and explored the dim interiors. Thousands of high-living spiders had also felt the breath of spring and were very much up and about. Their webs were spread everywhere. White-footed mice and bushy-tailed pack rats were scurrying here and there, busy at their spring housecleaning. Even the little striped chipmunks were awake, although still yawning and rubbing their sleepy eyes. There was no doubt that winter was past and spring was here.

It had been a cozy honeymoon for us, but we were not too sad now that it was over. Soon linemen would be up and we would have electric light and heat. The government snow shovel had already passed Nisqually bridge and was moving a half-mile a day along the valley road. The snow was settling more than a foot each day and Sluiskin Falls at the head of the valley had suddenly roared into new life. In Edith Creek Basin, where we had often skied and I had built a small jump, we discovered Edith Creek Canyon and Fairy Falls—they had been completely snowed under, and the falls silenced during the winter.

Here we got a good look at the graceful Alaska cedars *(Chamaecyparis nootkatensis)* which we had first seen on the ridge between the Nisqually and the Paradise Rivers. The dense yellow wood of this tree contains a volatile oil which discourages insect and fungus growth and so preserves the wood. It also gives it a pleasant odor. This oil is characteristic of all the so-called cedars. I say "so-called" because the name "cedar" as used in America is a misnomer more confused, even, than the Douglas fir.

I had learned in my dendrology classes at college that there are only four known species of the genus *Cedrus* which are the *true* cedars. These are the *atlantica,* or Atlas cedar of North Africa; the *libani,* or cedar of Lebanon; and the *deodara,* or deodar cedar of the Himalayan regions. The fourth is a little known species *brevifolia,* found on the island of Cyprus.

No other trees should be called "cedar," but our European ancestors have dubbed almost every tree "cedar" which has scale-like (rather than needle-like) leaves. Here in America there are a score or more species of half a dozen different genera ranging from *Juniperus* to *Chamaecyparis* that are mistakenly called cedars. Strangely enough, the true cedars all have needle-like leaves and resemble the larch more than the trees we call "cedar."

This Alaska yellow cedar, which grows at sea level in southern Alaska and only above three thousand feet in the northern Cascades, is more closely related to the cypresses of Europe. There are only six species of the genus, three of which grow in America and two of these on the West Coast. The other West Coast species is the magnificent Port Orford cedar, or Lawson's cypress, of the lower Oregon coast.

Thus men confuse their thinking in a futile attempt to simplify their knowledge.

2

DAILY NOW NEW TRACKS BEGAN to appear in the high country. The first marmots came cautiously out of hibernation, basked for an hour in the noonday sun, and went back into their dens for a final week's snooze before beginning a busy season of eating and loafing. Coyote and bobcat tracks became common, and there were thousands of lacy little trails made by mice, chipmunks, ground squirrels, weasels, birds, and even a few pioneering insects. Soon we saw our first deer—a shy young buck peering at us from the edge of a thicket of dwarf firs; and the next time we took the garbage cans to the dump we saw that bear had been there too. We figured from the freshness of the tracks and the apparent haste of their retreat that they had heard us coming and had just now dashed off down the hill. No doubt they were watching us from a safe place beyond some nearby cover.

Whether or not these bear realized that we were the waiters who served their free-lunch counter I do not know, but they came daily now and gradually became so bold that they would not leave the feast until we were almost upon them, and then they would reluctantly withdraw only a few yards and return again as soon as we left them alone.

With the awakening of the small winter sleepers, Paradise Inn itself came alive with nocturnal guests. Chipmunks and deer mice came into the kitchen and pantry; mantled ground squirrels rolled and frolicked in the pungent cedar sawdust of my dining room woodpile; weasels chased the rodents across our ceilings and through the attics; and pack rats began moving their chattels back and forth from room to room. In the daytime these were all interesting and amusing, but in the dead of night when we wished to sleep they were damnably annoying.

One night in early spring we heard a crash in the hotel kitchen that sounded to us as though a bear had broken in and was wrecking the place. When the din had stopped I lighted a lantern and went cautiously downstairs to investigate. But so far as I could see, everything was as it should be in the big unused kitchen. I looked behind stoves and under sinks and examined the doors and windows, but nothing appeared to be out of place. I went back to bed. Next night the same thing happened again, and we began to be frightened. We were sure now that it was not a bear or any other animal, but something we could not understand, and that was far worse than a whole family of bears.

Next day, however, on examining the kitchen more carefully, I found a window open a foot or so from the top, and ice which was slipping down the steep roof under pressure from snow above was curling beneath the eaves and into the room through this window. Under the window was a stack of big round-bottomed mixing bowls and other utensils used by the bakers for kneading dough and baking bread. Apparently small icebergs were breaking off from this miniature glacier and dropping at odd times into this stack of pots and pans, and the resulting crash was the noise we heard and magnified into such a commotion in the middle of the night.

Although they sometimes slept under the back stairs, bears never entered Paradise Inn so far as I know.

At Longmire Springs Gus Anderson had a more serious problem. Bears frequently burglarized National Park Inn, and although they did a great deal of damage, park regulations did not allow him to shoot them. One evening he put an electric coil in a bowl of bread and milk and set it out for one of the marauders. When bruin tentatively touched his nose to the "hot dish" he let out a roar, turned over backward in the air, lit on his feet like a cat, and as Gus said, "left so fast he made a hole in the night." But about a half-hour later Gus heard the heavy wire mesh being ripped off the pantry window again. The park rangers finally stepped into the picture. They made a trap out of a section of corrugated iron culvert, mounted it on a two-wheel trailer, and parked it conveniently and well baited by the kitchen door. The bear was easily trapped and the next day the trailer was hitched behind a pick-up truck, and bruin, squalling and muttering, was hauled twenty miles out along the Westside road. There in the uninhabited wilderness he was paroled. But it took him only about a week to get back to Longmire Springs.

Gus had problems with elk also. When he went out to inspect the outlying hotel cabins one day in early spring, he noticed that the door to one of them was open. When he approached, a yearling elk came out and ran away. Gus looked inside. Apparently the elk had used the cabin as shelter all winter. He had actually been sleeping on the bed, and the place looked and smelled more like a neglected stable than a hotel room.

3

NEAR THE END OF JUNE WE WENT OUT one morning and heard above the hooting of the sooty grouse and the roar of Sluiskin Falls a new sound. It came from far down the valley and we recognized it immediately as the hiss of steam and the clank of machinery. We quickly fastened on our skis and schussed down the trail. The Park Service road crew, with a steam shovel and plows, was opening the mountain road for the season's travel, and they were now on the switchbacks above Narada Falls. The snow was settling very fast and had become extremely hard to move. We stood on the lip of the cut and looked down at the big shovel gnawing away at the white mass of the mountain, reminded of a small, but very ambitious, mouse nibbling at the side of a huge layer cake. The snow was so hard that it was possible for the big machine (which weighed about fifteen tons) to roll over the surface of snow more than ten feet deep without sinking in, and so tough that the scarified lip of the half-yard bucket could only scrape the surface of the cut, like a child licking noisily at an ice cream cone.

The men also had heavy road plows which they would haul out in front of the shovel, then with a winch and cable haul them back while two men wrestled the plow to keep it in the icy snow. While we watched, they broke the beam out of one of the plows and trucked it back to the shops at Longmire to be repaired. Later they tried blasting the snow.

Following the war the army had given many tons of war-surplus powder to the National Park Service for construction uses. Actually it was TNT in the stick form used in big guns during the First World War. It was powerful and dangerous to work with because it was easily detonated

Steam shovel in spring

and the men were not too familiar with its use. We noticed that the old "powder monkey," who handled fistfuls of dynamite sticks as carelessly as so much cord wood and crimped dynamite caps with his teeth, handled this stuff with great respect, as one does something that is mysterious and unknown. When charges were set just before noon we moved well back and waited.

After the crew shut down the shovel, piled in the trucks, and started down the road for lunch at the camp they had set up at Narada Falls, the powderman stayed behind to set off the blast. We stayed to watch the show. This powder had cost the Service nothing and the supply seemed unlimited, so he was using it freely. During the morning he had set a dozen or more charges in "coyote holes" dug close together in the snow and ranging for a hundred yards up the road.

When all was clear the powderman called "Powderrrr" and from shelter behind the shovel plunged down the handle of the electric detonator. We moved back a step, although we were already ten times as far away as the powderman, and watched a great white curtain of snow rise slowly and silently into the air. An instant later the sound and shock wave struck us and almost knocked us over; but when we skied down, with the fine snow still settling out of the air, we saw that a trough blackened at the edges by the powder, but only a few yards wide and deep, had been blown in the snow. Hard ice would have been easier to move. Later it was found that the blasting actually did more damage to the rock-ballasted roadbed ten feet below than it did to the snow, and the use of explosives has been discontinued. Now powerful rotary snowplows pushed by heavy trucks keep the Paradise Valley road open all winter and thousands of skiers enjoy the powder snow and thrilling scenery of the high slopes.

Day by day the sound of the shovel grew closer, and soon from the inn we could see the clanking, stuttering machine slowly creeping up the deep trough it was gnawing through the layers of snow.

When it reached the upper valley early in July and was opposite us, the cut was so deep that we could not see the cab of the big shovel at all, but only the staggered puffs of smoke and steam from its exhaust. Its black, skeletal arm, and the bucket like a knotty fist at the end, reached up out of the depths and deposited handfuls of snow alongside the roadway, then disappeared again. After a period of muffled wheezing and snorting the arm would appear again with another handful of snow.

In the meantime an advance crew of hotel employees hiked in over the trail from Narada Falls and started putting the place in shape for the sudden rush of visitors which would come immediately when the road was declared open for public use.

T. H. Martin, the general manager of the hotel company, telephoned from Longmire early that morning and asked if Ruth could prepare a simple lunch for about twenty-five men. By this time she had solved most of the mysteries of high-altitude cookery, and while I stoked fires and opened cans, she pared potatoes, soaked dried fruits, baked a big ham, and whipped up a devil's food cake and five lemon meringue pies. It was a good dinner and the men had appetites to match it. Our kitchen that day reminded us of the harvest dinners we both had known on the farm. Although these men were clerks, cooks, bakers, carpenters, electricians, and plumbers, their *modus operandi* at the dinner table was quite comparable to that of hungry farm hands.

Harry Poppajohn, the rotund and jovial chef, and Nels Haugen, the head baker, took over immediately after dinner. They almost carried Ruth and me out of the kitchen, and began washing the dishes themselves before starting on the huge job of getting their kitchen and bakeshop back into commercial operation. Mr. Martin took time to put a friendly arm around Ruth and thank her. He was, when he chose to be, a real gentleman of the Southern school, and he treated us like a son and daughter, although sometimes when he was crossed, his anger flared like a Rebel yell and he could piece as choice an assortment of cusswords together in as fluent a manner as any top sergeant of the army ever aspired to.

Ruth and I spent the afternoon moving our things into a guest room, and at dinner that evening we sat down in the candle-lighted dining room as the first guests of the season.

The next day was Sunday, July 4; and we celebrated it by cheering the government road crew and the weary steam shovel around the last bend. They arrived in front of the inn about four in the afternoon—and directly behind the government trucks came the big red buses of the Park Company. The first ones were filled with college girl waitresses and maids, college boy guides, bellboys, busboys, tent boys, dishwashers, and sundry other helpers. Then not a hundred yards behind this bus there were two busloads of tourists. Most years it is earlier, and some years it is later (once the road was not open until July 17), but every year this is the pattern of spring arrivals, a human migration as regular as that of the birds and the bears.

So the place swarmed with people and activity. The road crew began shoveling snow away from the dining room windows and digging a long tunnel from the turnaround to the hotel entrance. This tunnel stood up until almost the end of July, although I must admit that hotel employees spread tarps over it at night to slow its melting, and thus maintain it as a novelty for the visitors from the sweltering lowlands.

That evening Ruth and I went down with the last bus, and for the first time in six months she set her feet on bare, dry ground again.

We had only a day's leave with our friends in Seattle, then Tuesday morning we headed up the hill again. This time Ruth was again a housewife, but I was a mountain guide.

4

OVER THIS FOURTH OF JULY WEEKEND other spectacular changes had taken place on our mountain. The first patch of bare ground had appeared on the south slope of Alta Vista, and the first creamy-white avalanche lilies were nodding a welcome to us and the warm spring sunshine.

Paradise Inn, so recently our home, was now a place unknown to us. Huge fires were roaring in the lobby fireplaces. In the dining room, where our woodpile had been, tables were set with spotless linen and gleaming silver; and where for months my lantern had cast dark shadows in deserted halls, there were now blazing lights and happy people. The place swarmed like a hive of bees.

Ruth and I quickly retrieved our personal effects and climbed the ridge to where crews of workmen were erecting scores of tent frames into what would be Camp of the Clouds—an overflow area for Paradise Inn. The crew foreman gave us a tent, showed us the lumber pile and the toolhouse, and we set about building our home for the summer.

It was a pleasant home, situated under a clump of alpine firs at the edge of the camp. There was a small stream nearby, and as soon as the snow had melted, acres of wild flowers all around us. We could not see the mountain from our door, but instead looked out across the valley to the Tatoosh Range on the south. Between two peaks of the rugged Tatoosh we could see the flat snow dome of Mount Adams, a sister peak to Mount Rainier, which stands some fifty miles to the southeast.

First we dug away the few feet of remaining snow and laid a solid board floor with low side walls. Over this we erected an eight-by-ten tent with fly. Another fly provided outdoor working and lounging space. I also built some tables and benches and swung a hammock between two nearby trees. We were soon as snug as the ground squirrel which promptly set up housekeeping under our floor and fought all night with his wife; or the pair of gray jays who lived somewhere in the branches above us and daily raided our table for food.

Each day now was a new miracle. I do not believe in "miracles," but they were happening all around us. People are inclined to call the things they see going on every day *natural* things, the things they think they understand, and those things that are unknown and mysterious to them *supernatural* or miraculous things. I prefer to call all things *natural,* for actually there is a vast amount that is unknown in the most familiar of daily happenings. I would not presume to divide the world into two parts on the basis of my ignorance or the lack of my understanding. The unborn child which we had already accepted as a present member of our family; the stars which looked down upon us at night and seemed closer and more intimate here in the clear upper air; the lovely alpine flowers which despite their innocence and delicacy are driven by such an urge to blossom and bear fruit that they push their buds up through three or four inches of snow at the edge of the snowbanks and actually bloom before the snow has melted away; the myriad insects and birds and animals who after the long winter stagnation were now bursting with energy and ambition; and even the running water which we heard all around us—these things were all natural and familiar, but they were miracle enough for us. To us there was only one world, a marvelous natural world, and we two felt very much a part of it.

5

I THINK THE MOST INDELIBLE MEMORY I have of that spring in Paradise Valley is of running water. Just as snow and silence had dominated the design for winter, so water and the sound of water dominated the spring. We noticed it as soon as we returned to the valley that Tuesday morning. Washington Cascades, where the road crosses and recrosses them above Narada Falls, had broken through the snow and were so deliriously free and so swollen with new life that they playfully drenched our bus at each bridge and drowned out all other sounds in the valley with their gay laughter. Higher up we noticed that Sluiskin Falls were thundering, and all around us was the sound of wild waters. Across the Nisqually Glacier half a dozen high waterfalls sprang out from the rim of the canyon where none had existed before, and under the snowbanks at our door and along the trail to the camp store where we purchased supplies, the newly released waters were splashing and gurgling. Spring was setting free the waters winter had held captive too long, and each drop was plunging madly back to its mother, the sea.

As the spots of bare ground spread before our tent and dried in the warm July sun, new flowers appeared—not daily, but by the hour. First the erythronium lilies, of which there are two varieties on Mount Rainier, and then a hundred other delicate blossoms in quick succession. Second in abundance, and only hours behind the lilies, were the pasqueflowers, which we call Western anemone. Their furry, dew-silvered leaves were already green when the snow released them, and in a day's time they grew three inches tall and opened silver-haired flower buds. Next day the dollar-size, creamy-white flowers with golden centers were following the sun from its first appearance over Mazama Ridge until its setting behind the shoulder of the mountain to the west. Next morning they were facing Mazama Ridge again, waiting expectantly for the rising sun. By now the waxy-yellow petals of the Suksdorf's buttercup lined the little waterways; and the scarlet tufts of the Indian paintbrush formed spots of brilliant color among the avalanche lilies and the anemone.

Soon cigar-shaped fingers of tightly rolled, gray green leaves were thrust up here and there in the expanding flower fields and these quickly unfurled into the huge, parallel-veined leaves of the giant hellebore. Later tall stalks of green flowers would blossom out, the greenest flowers that I have ever seen, aside from some of the green swamp orchids which grow lower down in the valleys. One of these swamp orchids bears the descriptive

Left: Avalanche lilies growing and blooming through several inches of snow. The alpine summer is so brief that flowers must crowd the spring in order to mature seeds before autumn snows. (Photo by L. D. Lindsley)

Below: Within a week after the snow has melted the hillsides are covered with fields of Erythronium, locally called "avalanche lily" because white masses like avalanches of snow flow down the hillsides. (Photo by L. D. Lindsley)

Avalanche lilies. (Photo by L. D. Lindsley)

species name of *viridifolia* (green-flowered). The hellebore is more closely related to the lilies than to the orchids.

Everywhere there appeared the yellow cinquefoil, which people confuse with the buttercups; and in the wetter places, often in water up to their sepals, stood the ranks of waxy-white marsh marigolds. Tiny veronica or speedwell gave dainty touches of the deepest blue; and pink miner's lettuce, or claytonia, spread like grass across the drier areas. Sitka valerian, called mountain heliotrope because of its fragrant heliotrope-like odor, quickly lifted its dense umbels of pinkish flowers over the hillside and gave us a sweet new odor which pervaded the entire valley. Along the Paradise River and Edith Creek an entirely different community of flowers burst into bloom. This aquatic community was dominated by the scarlet Lewis monkey flower and the yellow alpine mimulus, dainty flowers with simian faces which give reason for both the common name of "monkey flower" and the generic name of *Mimulus.* There are three or four other species of mimulus found in the park and they are all members of that large figwort or snapdragon family, which includes the attractive (in spite of its name) louseworts, the brilliant red painted cup or Indian paintbrush, the purple and scarlet elephant's-trunk and duck-billed cliff-dwelling pentstemons, and the blue-eyed veronica or speedwell.

Here also the heart-shaped leaves of the *Caltha* or marsh marigold sent up succulent stems to bear its creamy-white, golden-hearted flowers, and the cyclamen-like shooting star provided a pleasant contrast in reds and purples. Later in the summer one of my favorite flowers, the slender-stemmed grass of Parnassus *(Parnassia)* which grew beside the streams, bore snow-white buds which opened their fringed petals into half-inch floral creations that defy my description.

No place on earth except in a few similar alpine settings can you find such gorgeous wild flower gardens as along the streams of Paradise Valley: white water singing songs, gray water ouzels building nests, and massed flowers nodding approval—a combination of sounds, sights, and odors that lacks only an Adam and an Eve to make of it a little Garden of Eden within the larger Paradise. One other thing may be missing—warmth. The breezes off the glaciers may be a bit sharp and the alpine nights a mite cool for an Adam and Eve sans clothes, or only a wardrobe of fig leaves! And also there are mosquitoes.

As soon as the streams were open the water ouzel or dipper moved into the upper valley and began rearing their amphibious young. These are amazing little birds, somewhere between the warblers and the wrens in size and relationships and quite like the European ousel (the English dislike the "z") in general appearance. The European ousel is more brightly colored in browns, grays, and whites, but it has a similar song and the same aquatic habits.

There is another bird in northern Europe called the ring ousel, which is a thrush and totally unrelated to the little wrenlike "dipper."

Water ouzels have been reported from Paradise Valley in midwinter and I had seen and heard them all along the Nisqually River as I went back and forth to Longmire, but the first pair we saw in the high valley were building a nest below Sluiskin Falls in early July. I could not tell male from female by their looks, but they were obviously well paired for the job they had to do. Both were working frantically, carrying green moss to weave an oven-like structure about six inches in diameter with a

Pigmy Owl

two-inch entrance hole in one side. It was attached to a wet rock so close to the foot of the falls that water constantly splashed over it, and in late afternoon on warm days when the river swelled with the melting ice, it was completely hidden behind the falls. Later in the season when I had guide parties to the ice caves under the Stevens Glacier we would stop by the falls and watch the ouzels work. They had young by then and both birds were busy going and coming with the larvae of caddis flies and other water-breeding insects upon which they fed.

It is almost beyond belief, even when you see it, that a land bird can be so much at home in such turbulent waters. They can't even swim!

Usually we would spot one of the pair perched on a stone in midstream a bit below the falls. He would bob up and down a few times, wink his eye at us, and then walk off the rock into several inches of swift-flowing water and ramble around on the bottom as unconcernedly as a chicken in a barnyard. Apparently they clutch the bottom with their claws, for when they find a fat grub they seem to let go and bounce to the surface like a cork. Then they flutter to the nearest exposed rock, bob up and down a few times, and fly to a rock near the nest. After a cautious look around they dart behind the falls, passing through the spray at its edge, and disappear into the green ball of the nest. Apparently they build of living mosses which are kept alive and green by the spray of the waterfall. At other sites I have seen the nests attached to mossy ledges only inches above the rushing water of the river, where they must be in constant danger of being submerged or even torn away.

Almost equally startling as their "aqua follies" is their habit of singing cheerfully on dull winter days when all the other birds, except the chickadees, are huddling in the best shelter they can find. I was often cheered by

White-tailed ptarmigan with chicks

their wrenlike song as I trudged up the Nisqually trail with my mail and supply pack on my back.

As spring advanced into mid-July many other birds came into the high valleys to compete with the jays, ravens, and crows who had wintered there. Most beautiful were the pale, sky-blue, mountain bluebirds who built nests in cavities or woodpecker holes which they found in dead trees. They are of the same size and the same gentle ways as the common Western bluebird (which is rarely seen in the park) and they are the bluest of all bluebirds. The Steller's blue jays also moved up in numbers and contested the range with the gray jays and the Clark's crows. In fact, blue jays contest everything with everybody. We often saw them in front of our tent quarreling with the chipmunks and ground squirrels over nuts or the fat rich cones of the white-barked pine—or just quarreling.

Pipits, rosy finches, and pine siskins increased in numbers, and wrens moved into the stables and outhouses. There were swallows and nighthawks in the evening sky; and hawks, owls, and eagles were more frequently seen. The ptarmigan were mottled gray and white now, like barred rock hens, and they had already hatched their walnut-sized chicks. These followed their mothers about in the heather and grass at timberline and even out upon the snowfields, where I saw them picking up the insects that are carried there by the high winds. There the bugs are numbed by the cold and kept in cold storage for the birds.

At Reflection Lake I saw a pair of harlequin ducks fishing, and Ranger Flett told me that he found a pair nesting on a sand bar of the Nisqually River near Longmire. The rufous sides and black head with numerous white bars and patches cause this duck to stand out as one of the most strikingly colored birds I know.

The most conspicuous spring migrants, by far, were the woodpeckers. Perhaps this was because there were some dead fir snags just behind our tent which seemed to attract them like a magnet. Although the weathered snags must have been almost barren of food, I think the woodpeckers all came at one time or another to drum upon them. They often woke us too early in the morning with their raucous squawking and their incessant drumming. There were the small Gairdner woodpecker (the Pacific Coast

Sapsucker

form of the downy), the Harris, which is similar to the hairy of the east; and the Alaska three-toed and Sierra who somewhat resemble them. There

Pileated woodpecker

were noisy, red-shafted Northwestern flickers, who look and act like the common flicker but have brilliant red under the wings instead of lemon yellow, and beautiful red and black Northern sapsuckers, who bore rows of small holes around the trunks of living trees—not to eat the resinous sap as their name would indicate, but to set traps for greedy insects which are attracted by the flow of sap and then caught in its sticky gum. These uniformly spaced rows of holes, and the heavy welts on the trees caused by them, are conspicuous on Alaska yellow cedar trees in the valley. New to me and strangest of all was the iridescent greenish-black Lewis woodpecker with its red face and rose-tinted belly, and the big red-crested, jet-black, pileated woodpecker or logcock. Most of these are year-round residents of the area but, like the bear and the deer, they migrate vertically a few thousand feet with the changing seasons.

Two hummingbirds also appeared with the first scarlet flowers of the wild currant—the relatively large rufous (three and one half inches long) and the tiny (in fact the smallest U.S. hummingbird) calliope. The rufous we had known around Seattle, but the calliope is found only in the high mountains. Aside from the fact that the calliope is only about half as big as the rufous, the two can be distinguished readily by the iridescent green upper parts of the calliope in contrast with the reds of the rufous. The males of both species have fiery red gorgets, or throat patches. Since it has no song, I presume that the name of this tiny feathered dynamo comes from that of the Greek Muse who presides over eloquence and poetry rather than from the well-known instrument of musical torture, the steam calliope.

During the spring and summer we also saw numerous herons, blackbirds, wild pigeons, thrushes, warblers, vireos, creepers, kinglets, juncos, towhees, pigmy owls, and robins, in addition to those already mentioned. A total of 102 species of birds is listed by the Biological Survey (now the U.S. Fish and Wildlife Service) in the park.*

Bears began to be more conspicuous as those from the lower forests worked their way into the upper valleys, in anticipation, no doubt, of the fields of blueberries, already in bloom, which later would spread across the hillsides a feast irresistible to bears and Indians (and, as it turned out, Ruth).

6

ON MY TRIPS TO LONGMIRE (after spring had already arrived at that elevation), I had become acquainted with a certain brown mother bear whom we later called Avalanche Lily. I saw her first near an old mining claim about a mile above the Springs. She was coming up the trail followed by two small cubs. She seemed to be familiar with men and to have learned that park men would not harm her. She was not so sure, however, what they might do to her new cubs. When we came face to face in the trail we both stopped, and the cubs, one straw-colored and the other

---

* One-hundred-seventy-one species of birds are now listed by the U.S. Fish and Wildlife Service.

Blackie and Avalanche Lily. (Photo by Rounds)

The bear came into the hole and I got out. . . . the hole wasn't big enough for both of us. (Photo by Floyd Schmoe)

jet-black, crowded between their mother's shaggy legs. We silently questioned each other a moment, and she was still not willing to take chances with her cubs, so she ordered them to climb a tall fir tree beside the trail. They scurried up and did not stop until they came to the first branches some forty feet above the ground. Then she came back up the trail. I stood my ground as long as I dared, then got off the trail and she went past me. After watching the cubs for a few minutes (they were watching their mother depart and whimpering to themselves), I went on down to Longmire.

When I returned an hour or so later the cubs were not in the tree and the family was nowhere in sight. On one or two other occasions I saw them in the lower valley, and Heinie Evans at the mining claim told me that they were old friends of his. He had known the mother for several years.

One evening when the snow had nearly all melted from around our camp, I returned late from the guidehouse to find Ruth not in the tent. Soon I heard her call from behind the camp. There was a certain suppressed urgency in her voice which made me hurry to her. She was backed up against the dead fir trees clutching them with her hands. Ten feet up Blackie, the brunet cub, peered cautiously around one of the trees. Brownie was perched on a broken branch a few feet up another dead snag, and the angry mother bear sat facing Ruth. Avalanche Lily and her cubs had arrived in Paradise. Ruth was between her and her cubs (which she thought was bad), and she was between Ruth and the tent (which was bad). When I came around the tent she turned her head to look at me but did not budge from her post of duty.

With no weapon in my hand, I hesitated to start a rear-guard diversionary action (the old gal weighed at least four hundred pounds and she was not happy about anything). I was afraid to advise Ruth to retreat without diversion, as the bear might mistake any movement on her part as an unfriendly action toward the cubs. It looked like a stalemate which could not be maintained indefinitely.

Fortunately, some tourists who were passing by saw the bears and gathered around to watch the show. The mother bear became more agitated as the situation became more involved. Her attention was now divided, but she held her ground. I moved over on the opposite side and motioned Ruth to come slowly in my direction. It was Avalanche Lily's move now, and she took the position Ruth had vacated. The tourists advanced to photograph the family group, and we beat a dignified retreat.

Ruth told me that she had been "treed" for what seemed like an hour. She had heard a commotion in back of the camp and had gone to investigate. She saw the two innocent-looking little cubs up the trees but had failed to notice their mother, who had gone farther along to investigate the garbage can situation. With a mother's instinct Ruth had gone to the foot of the trees to comfort the cubs, who appeared to her to have been abandoned. When she looked around mama was there—and there she stayed until I came.

For the next several weeks Avalanche Lily and her cubs were a major tourist attraction in Paradise Valley, and as the cubs grew larger and bolder the mother bear grew less sensitive about them. They were not afraid of people and managed to make a very good living as wandering mendicants. The mother usually kept discreetly in the background.

I had another close brush with a bear a week or so later. I had carried our garbage can to the pits below the camp and after dumping it there I walked on down the trail. Soon I met a bear coming up. He was a huge black brute walking slowly with his head low. Apparently he did not yet see me. I had my camera along, as there were frequently bear around the garbage pit and I had hoped to get some good pictures. This looked like the shot I wanted.

There was a deep hole beside the trail where the trail crew had been digging material for a fill, so I jumped down into it, hoping to get a picture as the bear went by me. But he did not go by. Instead he came into the hole with me. I think I must have smelled like garbage. I got a good picture of bruin against the sky just as he started in—and just before I started out. I figured there was not room enough in that hole for both of us.

7

ON LONG SUNNY DAYS WHILE I WAS OUT with guide parties, Ruth lay in the hammock by our camp and enjoyed the passing scene. There was always activity at the big hotel a few hundred yards below her: cars coming and going; people starting out on hikes or wandering over the flower-covered slopes; guide parties equipped with heavy boots, ropes and ice axes starting for the summit or to explore one of the nearby glaciers; horses at the corral in front of the inn, or horse parties mounting for the Skyline Trail trip, or outfitting for longer expeditions; and rangers in Stetson hats and the forest-green uniform of the National Park Service going about their various duties—a busy scene, with the backdrop always of the rugged Tatoosh Range and sleepy Mount Adams beyond.

People often dropped by to chat with us—friendly if curious people who were enjoying their visit on the mountain. They often wanted to see the inside of our tent and to ask questions about our life. We were glad to have them come, but we sometimes felt as though we were considered one of the "exhibits," to be classed with the chipmunks, the bears, and the flowers. We both learned much about human nature from them and we often sat back and talked about them, as monkeys in a zoo must discuss their visitors. Most of course were decent intelligent people, but there were always conversation pieces among them. The courteous, well-informed people who asked sincere questions and obviously enjoyed all they saw and did were a joy to know, and not infrequently we cross trails with some of them even today. I think there was something about the setting which gave depth to these contacts, much as the warm lights and spacious quietness of a well-designed art gallery add depth to a fine painting. Then too, these people, the more discerning of them, were in the process of being recharged, resensitized, by the majesty of the scene around them, and such a phenomenon in process must, like the process of charging a battery, give off some warmth that can be felt by others nearby.

Although they may not give logical reasons to their actions, many people are drawn to the wildernesses of nature because of an unspoken need to recapture something lost from their lives. It is perhaps that man has become too "civilized." He has breathed civilization's air too long, endured its noises, borne its burdens—they have exhausted him. To find recreation for body, mind, and soul he must need return sometimes to the wilderness from whence he came. Fortunately there are many great wildernesses like those of Mount Rainier still to be found on earth—there are forests, plains, deserts, and the infinite sea. And if a man cannot handily reach any of these he has only to look upward, and there, ever close at hand although unbelievably far away, is the vast wilderness of the sky. There is a balm in Gilead. People who feel this common need share a bond if the mood is right, even in casual meetings.

There were others of course too shallow, or too empty (at the moment) to impress us with more than their emptiness. Of these we remember only their foolish questions and remarks, and not them as people. They asked us if we always lived like this, and they asked Ruth how she could stand being so far away from "everything." For foolish questions we often had foolish answers, like the time the fellow asked one rainy day, "Does it always rain up here?" and I answered, "No, sometimes it snows."

The people we could not understand at all were those who came to the inn with its surrounding carpet of wild flower fields and the huge backdrop of tumbling ice and soaring rock and sat all day with their backs to it, drinking and playing cards. Ignorantly empty people may be endured but intelligent people who are deliberately empty are insufferable.

But our happiest neighbors were the gray jays, the chipmunks, and the ground squirrels. These became very tame and would take food from our hands. A pair of golden-mantled ground squirrels lived under our tent, and almost every safe cranny in the fallen trees or broken stumps housed a family of chipmunks. The gray jays had nested earlier in the dense clumps of trees, and so secretly that I never discovered their nests.

When she had nothing better to do, Ruth would tease the ground squirrels by tying a nut on the end of a string and dragging it away when they reached for it. If they caught it they would clutch it with both front paws and dig in their heels to hold. She would drag them around this way, then snatch the nut away and dangle it over their heads. They would stand up on their hind feet and reach for it like a cat playing with a spool on a string. When she placed a nut on her hammock rope they climbed up the tree trunk and walked out on the rope to get it. Seeing this, she devised a really sadistic trick. She tied a choice nut on the end of a string and hung it from the hammock rope just out of reach from the ground. The ground squirrels walked around on their hind feet for a few minutes trying to reach the dangling nut, and then one of them figured it out correctly. He climbed up the tree and ran out on the rope to the string. He then reached down and hauled up the string hand over hand until he had the nut. He had already learned that nuts cannot be plucked from strings, so he cut the string with his teeth, scampered down the tree, and disappeared with a flirt of his bushy tail under the tent floor. There the happy pair stored nuts and cones and other bits of surplus food for the family of little ground squirrels that was in prospect.

These friendly animals, who grow fat and sleek on tourist handouts, are always amusing. It was fun just to sit in the door of the tent and watch them come and go, often with their cheek pouches so filled with nuts and seeds that they appeared to be suffering from a bad case of double mumps. Apparently they had fleas, as most animals do, so they loved dust baths

Mantled ground squirrels

and the area in front of the tent, which Ruth swept daily, was a good place in which to roll and stretch. Their sanitation was also their pleasure, and they scuffled and rolled in the dust like a pair of small boys. Sometimes they would turn somersaults, roll over and over, flatten out on their backs with their round, well-filled stomachs up and stretch. There is real comfort and physical joy in a good leisurely stretch. Then they would flatten out on their bellies, chins on the ground, and push themselves along with their hind feet. After a dust frolic they would jump up, shake themselves well, and scamper off as though it gave them great satisfaction.

Biologists have given the mantled ground squirrel a really terrific name, *Callospermophillus lateralis saturatus,* which according to my Latin dictionary would mean "the beautifully adorned, prolific one, who has stripes on his side and a full belly"—although it could mean, by the same dictionary, "the thick-skinned seed lover, who has fancy flanks and a full belly." I notice that a more recent text has changed it to *Citellus saturatus,* simply "the full-bellied ground squirrel." Biologists with a yen for nomenclature sometimes do this sort of thing, not for any scientific reason but simply, it seems, to amuse themselves.

8

THE MOUNT RAINIER GUIDE STAFF that year was, in my opinion, a top-notch organization. There were eight men and one woman on the team, most of them college people, but the excellence of the service was due largely to the ability and leadership of one man, Hans Fuhrer, the chief guide.

Hans, who came from a long line of guides in Switzerland—so long that the family name had become Führer (guide)—is one of the most powerful men I know. He is some six feet two in height, two hundred pounds in weight, and all hard beef and bone from the toes of his huge feet to the tips of his bear-paw hands. Hans was already famous as a climber and he became almost equally famous for his yodeling. He is no mean hand at the accordion either. His given name was John, although few people knew it, and he came from a mountain village near Grindelwald in the Bernese Oberland. His father and grandfather were guides before him—in fact, there were so many guides in the area who were named "Fuhrer" that when Hans wrote to his father in Switzerland he had to address him as *John Hans Fuhrer, Husband of Greta Hensel, Grund Innert-kirchen,* et cetera, et cetera. Young Hans went through the rigorous apprenticeship of porter and assistant guide that is required before a Swiss mountain guide receives his certificate and *Führerbuch,* and he scaled the Matterhorn with his father when he was only nine years old.

Perhaps it was because there were too many guides in Switzerland, but more likely it was his adventurous spirit that caused Hans to come to America at the age of twenty-four. His first job was among Swiss dairy farmers in the Willamette Valley of Oregon, but the snowcapped summits of the nearby Cascades soon drew him back to his real love, mountaineering. During the next three years he led more than a hundred parties to the summit of Mount Hood and his name became well known in local mountaineering circles.

This was his second season on Rainier as chief guide for the National Park Company. It was a job for an entire staff of guides, so Hans had sent for his "little brother Heinie" to come out from Switzerland to help him. Heinie was two inches taller than Hans and just as heavy. During the six years they worked on Mount Rainier they each made more than 150 summit trips and guided some three thousand climbers to the top and back. Although five or six climbers lost their lives on the treacherous old mountain during that period, only one was lost from Hans' parties.

At about 11,500 feet elevation, where the glacier plunges down the headwall of the Nisqually Cirque, there is a treacherous icefall. The trail at this point is between the ice and the rock. It is called the Chutes.

Hans' party on that occasion was descending the Chutes and because it was a large slow party they were late. Rocks had begun to fall. Hans was hurrying the party as fast as safety permitted, but near the bottom of the Chutes, when most of the climbers were already in the shelter of Gibraltar Rock, a falling stone struck a young Stanford student, who was near the end of the line, killing him as though he had been struck by a cannon ball.

Hans was terribly broken up over the tragedy and blamed himself, although it was an unavoidable accident. He said he would quit guiding, and he did quit Rainier, but the next year he and Heinie were guiding for the Canadian Pacific Railway in the Canadian Rockies.

It was not until many years later, after he had led thousands of parties on hazardous climbs in all the high mountain regions of the West from Alaska to California, that Hans finally settled down with his wife Mary and their son Hans, Jr., on the long-planned-for dairy farm in Oregon,

Heinie and Hans Fuhrer, Swiss summit guides. At the extreme left, in background, is the log cabin where the author lived with his family. (Photo by Ranapar Studio)

but even now at seventy years of age Hans never misses an opportunity to get into the snow mountains for a bit of climbing. He is just tapering off gradually, he says.

Hans wasted no time that spring lecturing us on the art of mountaineering and guiding. He saw to it that we had the proper equipment and then took us immediately onto the glaciers and peaks. There we took turns chopping steps in ice, leading the party in, around and across crevasses, judging if we should or should not cross snow bridges, roping climbers up and down difficult rock, and ending up with a simulated rescue from the bottom of a deep crevasse. During the first week of the season we did all the scheduled guide trips, except the summit climb, with Hans and Heinie.

There is much to learn about mountain climbing and the safe han-dling of parties on rock and ice or in the violent storms that can blow up so quickly at high elevations, and a lot of it can only be learned by actual experience, but Hans taught us a very great deal of the fundamentals dur-ing that week. The mature judgment so very important to safety in the mountains would have to come with time.

With inexperienced climbers in groups of from two to thirty we would be doing none of the really difficult ice or rock climbs, so we spent no time on such technical devices as belaying or rappeling. Hans believed in *keeping* out of trouble, not *getting* out of trouble. His first consideration was equipment and "equipment" was primarily shoes. With Hans, shoes were basic in more ways than one. His own feet were so big that he had to have shoes made to order and he had them hand-made in Switzerland because he thought that only the Swiss mountaineers knew how to make proper mountain boots. The hand-forged *triconie* and edging nails were also imported from Switzerland but these he very carefully put in himself. If Hans could be found around the guidehouse at all it would most likely be in the equipment room working at the cobbler's bench, either on his own or Heinie's shoes or helping one of us with ours. Most of his time was spent on the mountain.

Next to shoes came socks. Hans always wore two pair of wool socks and carried an extra pair in his rucksack. Mary knitted his socks but Heinie had a girl friend back in Switzerland who also sent beautifully soft hand-knitted socks to him.

On long trips over summer snow, colored glasses are another very neces-sary piece of equipment. Snow blindness is an extremely painful thing. Even with the careful use of tinted glasses I injured my eyes that spring and summer so badly that after all these years I still suffer acutely from brilliantly reflected light. We also use white theatrical grease paint to protect our faces from sun-burn, usually putting a dab of black under the eyes to prevent glare.

Hans did not have much use for alpenstocks because some people are more likely to stumble over them than to use them to prevent stumbling, but the guidehouse supplied them and Hans let members of his parties use them if they wanted to. Only the guides carried ice axes except when some experienced climber brought his own ax with him. Hans had a friend in Grindelwald who forged his and he imported ice axes from Switzerland for the other guides also. I had brought one home with me the year before.

This was before the beautiful nylon ropes we have today were developed, and Hans also bought our climbing ropes in Switzerland. Each guide carried a rope suitable for the party he had and the climb they were on, but only with small parties in such dangerous spots as the Chutes did we actually tie climbers together. With a large group there was too much danger that one clumsy climber might drag the entire party into a crevasse or down a cliff, so the rope became only a sort of guard rail which we hung onto. We tried to keep the people out of places where there was too much danger. Still there was an added thrill and a bit of color to "roping up" on the glaciers and there was considerable safety in having a stout rope stretched between a string of amateur mountaineers crossing a yawning crevasse or a sheer cliff. It also had a psychological effect.

But do not let me give the impression here that it is perfectly safe to go wandering about on the glaciers and peaks of Mount Rainier National Park or any other similar area, or that the equipment and the precautions we took were primarily stage dressing to give the customer a thrill or a feeling of danger. During the time I worked on Mount Rainier as guide and ranger more than twenty-five people lost their lives in climbing accidents and in most cases it was because they did not take the simple precautions and exercise the care Hans taught us.

9

THERE WERE TWO GLACIER TRIPS and one rock climb which we regularly took out of Paradise Valley that summer besides the summit climb and a number of horse trips such as the Skyline Trail around the rim of the valley. These are still the most exciting trips in Paradise although now with the Nature Guide Service more people go on the free "flower walks" with the park naturalists.

On the Nisqually Glacier we climbed up the long slope before the inn and dropped down slightly to the rim of the Nisqually Canyon. At this point everyone was usually willing to sit down for a few minutes on the heather-covered slope and catch his breath while I pointed out some of the scenic features and told them something about the glacier. We had already climbed more than a thousand feet and were almost seven thousand feet above sea level. The summit of the mountain looked very close although it was still some five miles away. Over the Tatoosh Range to the south we could see two other beautiful snowcapped volcanic mountains: Mount St. Helens on the right and Mount Adams on the left. If the day was very clear we could see Mount Hood in Oregon between the two, more than a hundred miles away.

Seen through the gaps in the clumps of timberline trees along the canyon rim the Nisqually Glacier is an imposing sight. It is only about five hundred feet away but that five hundred feet are straight down. Looking to the right and the left we could see the entire expanse of the ice river from its source in the summit snows to its terminus far down the rock-walled canyon. Beyond the moraine-covered "snout" of the glacier we could see the roadway looping back and forth up the valley, and the bridge where it crossed the Nisqually River just below the ice.

The Nisqually is one of eight primary glaciers on Mount Rainier. By "primary" the geologist means glaciers that start at the summit and extend down the mountainside in an unbroken flow all the way to their ends. I have since had the rare pleasure of looking down upon this vast ice field, covering more than forty-five square miles, from twenty thousand feet in the air. From this height it looks very much like a giant white octopus or a starfish with the black rim of the volcanic crater forming an eye in its central body and its eight sinuous arms or rays reaching out in all directions into the dark forests which surround the mountain on every side. In between the arms of the octopus, sometimes as feeder glaciers to them, are a number of secondary glaciers. These, like the Wilson Glacier which we could see tumbling onto the Nisqually at a point just opposite us, usually originate in cirques at around ten thousand feet. There are a total of twenty-eight named glaciers on the mountain although technically it is sometimes difficult to distinguish between true glaciers and permanent or residual ice fields. By a dictionary definition a glacier is a river of ice which *moves* down a mountainside. It is quite certain that some of the so-called *dead* glaciers, like the Muir Icefield and the Paradise Glacier, no longer move and therefore should correctly be called ice fields.

But the Nisqually which we were going to explore is a *live* glacier. Surveys made over the past fifty years indicate that it is moving fifteen or twenty inches each summer day and there was evidence of this spread out below us in the broken face of the ice where it flows over ledges and humps in the rocky channel it has cut for itself into the side of the mountain, and in the curve downward of the lateral cracks and crevasses. This is an indication that a glacier, like a river of water, moves faster in midstream than at its edges, and for the same reason. The friction against the edges where ice meets rock holds back the flow on either side. There was audible evidence of movement also. On any still summer day, especially a warm one, you can hear the cracking and the groaning of the moving ice, and avalanches are often heard and sometimes seen along the upper steeper slopes where great masses of ice periodically break loose and crash down upon the slower-moving ice below.

The Nisqually at this point is about a half-mile wide and perhaps five hundred feet thick. On the surface of the lower reaches there is much rock and other debris carried there by wind and gravity from the precipitous cliffs on either side, but more abundantly by the plucking and scouring action of the ice itself as it undercuts the walls and, because of the more rapid movement in midstream, gradually swings the debris out onto the river of ice until the lower surfaces are entirely covered with rock. This rock, as the glacier at about four thousand feet elevation melts out from beneath it, forms the terminal moraine. There are also distinct lateral moraines where the glacier in its more aggressive youth pushed ridges of rock to either side. We would cross the left-hand moraine when we went down upon the ice. On the Nisqually there is also a medial moraine which I pointed out from its source as a lateral moraine of the tributary Wilson Glacier lying opposite and above us. This is a floating ridge of rock constantly moving down with the ice and contributing to the terminal debris.

There were usually a number of questions because this is an interesting and not too familiar phenomenon. Usually they were intelligent questions, but sometimes there were very strange ones. Often someone asked whether, if a person fell into a crevasse and the body were not recovered, it would eventually appear at the end of the glacier. This has happened in the Swiss Alps but it is likely that in an active glacier such as the Nisqually any object would be ground to bits long before it reached the end of the glacier. I told them I doubted it but that there were several bodies already imbedded in Rainier glaciers and we would only have to wait a few hundred years to see if they ever appeared again.

Those who had seen the milky-white waters of glacial streams in other areas and had noted the chalky color of the Nisqually when they had crossed it on the way up to Paradise Valley sometimes asked about the erosive action of the ice. Although glaciers have played a leading role in sculpturing mountains like the Alps and the Rockies and have been the chief tool in carving out such masterpieces as the Matterhorn and Yosemite Valley, the remnants of ice left in our Western mountains today are an almost negligible force in land erosion. I had read that geologists estimate that some twenty-five cubic miles of rock have been cut away from the mountain during the past few thousand years, chiefly by glaciers. I pointed out the truncated and fluted condition of the old volcanic stump before us and could indicate by the tilt of lava flows visible in Gibraltar Rock and other remnants of the original cone that the peak was once several thousand feet higher than it now is and far greater in bulk. I also called their attention to the broad gravel plain known as the Tacoma Prairies, across which they had driven on the way up, as the outwash from one segment of Mount Rainier.

Later, when I was Park Naturalist on the mountain, I took occasion one hot August day to collect a cubic foot of Nisqually River water and allow the sediment to precipitate. When the water was clear I poured it off, dried and weighed the rock flour, and found that I had ten and a half ounces of powdered rock. I estimated the flow at that time at about one hundred foot-seconds, which means that some one hundred cubic feet of water were moving past a given point each second. By multiplying ten and a half ounces by the amazing number of seconds to be found in twenty-four hours I discovered that some 170 *thousand tons* of rock were being carried away each summer day by this one stream. Multiply this by eight such streams and many smaller ones and you have a staggering total. It is then not difficult to believe that twenty-five cubic miles could be torn off and carried away during the thousands of years. This is no icy-breathed mouse gnawing away at the huge volcanic pile, or even a clanking steam shovel such as was used to open the Paradise road. Approximately ten cubic miles of granite were ground away and deposited as fertile soil along the Merced and San Joaquin Rivers to form the Yosemite Valley, and granite is a far harder rock than the agglomerates of Mount Rainier. Still so little ice is left in our Western mountains that the total effect, compared to other forms of erosion, is slight.

The trail leads down from the canyon rim through a magnificent field of wild flowers which, during the short season, changes from day to day with kaleidoscopic effect. From fields of white and yellow avalanche lilies interspersing the snowbanks, to creamy anemone, blue lupine, green hellebore, yellow cinquefoil and buttercups, scarlet pentstemon, blue veronica, and scores of other species, to the ultimate glory of the masses of purple heather, the pageant of spring moves up the mountainside. Here too we often saw unusual birds, a hen ptarmigan with her chicks, a pair of pallid horned larks scurrying about a patch of pumice, or a flock of tiny pine siskins wheeling over the moraine.

Reaching the moraine we had to scrabble up the steep slope of loose material to an unstable path along the ridge. Then we were close to the ice and could feel the cold radiating from it, but because the sliding rock constantly feeds onto the flowing ice it was impossible to see exactly where earth and ice met. Along the moraine few plants gain a foothold in the constantly shifting soil but there are always a few patches of the hardy Alaska spiraea *(Luetkea pectinata)* with yellowish flower stalks only two or three inches high, and dense mats of mountain phlox *(Phlox diffusa)* so covered with dime-size blue flowers that the mosslike leaves are completely hidden beneath. There are marmots here also and families of conies, and on the cliff opposite near the hanging ice of the Wilson Glacier I could often point out a family of mountain goats scrambling up to a cool resting place or, if the time was midafternoon, lying on the snow-covered ice to get away from the heat and the flies of their feeding grounds below.

Summer flower field in Paradise Valley. Purple asters in foreground with a mass of blue lupine and the silver-gray seed heads of the western anemone beyond. Alpine firs on the ridge. These are a few of the more than five hundred species of flowers which bloom on Mount Rainier during the brief season. (Photo by L. D. Lindsley)

Because of the unstable nature of the moraine, which is composed of loose material ranging from pumice and volcanic ash to great lava boulders as big as a truck, we had to pick our way very carefully down the hundred-foot slope to the safer ice. Here a step might cause an avalanche and every move had to be carefully guarded. I have at times found myself on shifting morainal material standing almost at the exact margin of stability where I was afraid to move in any direction. In this situation it is usually best, if possible, to scramble straight up the slope and hope to outrun the falling rocks.

Once safely on the ice the party was usually awed by the imminence of the towering walls of ice and rock above them and by the tumbled wilderness of broken ice around them. Where it was safe to approach the first narrow crevasses closely, I would ask them to listen while I dropped a small stone down into the crack. It could be heard to tinkle back and forth as it fell until finally the sound faded in the depths of green ice.

Here we would "rope up" and, moving very slowly, I would cut wide, safe steps up a soaring ridge of ice between huge, apparently bottomless crevasses on either side until we reached the white central dome of the glacier. Standing there was like standing at the crest of a huge frozen cataract. This is a place for awe and wonder but there is danger that it will become overwhelming. Several times I had women in my party who went this far without protest and then, in the middle of a no man's land of ice, were overcome with fear and apprehension and refused absolutely to take another step in any direction. Sometimes this was a problem for a psychologist rather than a guide, and although I had never studied psychology I had learned some.

The first rule was to keep them on their feet. If they ever sat down it was difficult to get them up again. Next, find something to relieve the tension and distract the mind. Anything to get their eyes off those yawning crevasses. There are nice echoes here and Hans with his yodeling could inspire or divert the most hysterical female, but all I could do was yell and start others calling and listening. A good laugh could sometimes be induced from others in the party by such mountain wit as: "Brother, if you slip here, slip both ways," or "Go easy . . . , glacier poisoning . . . one drop kills," and laughter, being contagious, sometimes relieved tensions. Hans had another technique at which I was not so good. That was to scoop the woman up in his arms, toss her over his shoulder and carry her down bodily. Some women liked this, once they recovered from the initial shock,

The author. (Photo by L. D. Lindsley)

and I think Hans liked it too because once he packed a girl who had fallen and hurt her ankle all the two miles back to the guidehouse. On this occasion I was second guide on the party and the girl was not too heavy or too unlovely a burden so that I offered at several points to spell Hans for a way but he seemed never to get tired. The doctor said it was only a minor sprain and she undoubtedly could have hobbled in with much less help.

My final resort in such cases was to pull up on the rope, say, "Come on now, we're going down," and keep on going. The lady always came along.

Going back up the moraine one day I had a very close call. The path passed beneath a huge angular boulder higher than my head. I laid my hand on it in passing and felt it move. I yelled "Stop!" to the man behind me and leaped ahead. The rock brushed the seat of my pants as it crashed down upon the ice and rolled for a hundred yards until it landed in a crevasse. It was fortunate that I had unroped at the edge of the ice or we might all have been dragged down with the rock.

10

ON THE STEVENS GLACIER TRIP the caves and the "nature coasting" were the features. The Nisqually trip was thrilling and educational; the Stevens Glacier trip was just a lot of fun. There was a long easy hike across Edith Creek Basin and along Paradise River, then up Mazama Ridge, past Sluiskin Falls and beyond timberline, where we crossed the Paradise snow fields which are the source of Paradise River. The Stevens Glacier beyond is a "dead" ice field in that it lies in a high cirque and does not flow down the mountain as the great primary glaciers do. Therefore there are no large crevasses and no floating rock and it is safe to hike and slide almost anywhere on the snow and ice. In early season it is covered all over with snow and it is then necessary to dig an entrance into the ice caverns at its snout.

Where the streams emerge from the terminus of the glacier and where they flow under it they melt away the ice. This melting is speeded by currents of warm air entering where the stream emerges and flowing up along the waterways. Caverns larger than railway tunnels are melted under the ice and they can be followed sometimes for miles. They change somewhat from year to year, and no one has ever explored them all. We took parties only a few hundred yards into the caverns. It was strangely beautiful inside as the sunlight filtering through the ice and snow above is changed into rainbow colors, and it is not dangerous so long as one is careful not to pass under the flakes of ice that sometimes split away from the sides and top of the cavern. We never had any trouble, but a tourist who visited the caves without a guide poked at one of these hanging ice masses with his alpenstock to see if it would fall. It did—and killed him.

On the usual half-day guide trip we always made a long circle on the glacier and had several slides of two or three hundred feet as well as many shorter ones. On the short steep slopes we sent people down singly with a

The author inside one of the great ice caverns under the Paradise Glacier. The sunlight filtering through a hundred feet of solid ice is changed to beautiful tints of green, blue, and pink. The Paradise River is "born" here. (Photo by Floyd Schmoe)

guide at the bottom to pick them up, but on long gentle slopes we all sat down with each man holding the feet of the one behind him. When all were ready the guide in front would lift his feet and the guide behind would shove off and the entire party would serpentine down the glacier whooping and yelling. It was good sport and no one was ever hurt much.

On the Stevens I could sometimes find glacier worms and exhibit them to my party. There was always doubt that animal life could exist on the glaciers and utter disbelief that ice and snow were the preferred habitat of even a worm. Actually these dark brown earthworm-like annelids are abundant at around seven thousand feet on the icefields of Rainier but they can only be found at the surface on dull or cloudy days. The sunshine is either too warm or too desiccating to suit their comfort. So on bright days I never mentioned glacier worms unless someone asked about them. This they often did and if I could not produce the worms there was outright disbelief. But on dark days at the melting edge of the snow, along the dirty fringe where this season's snow was melting back from last season's snow (which was now ice) and where a trace of wind-blown dust and volcanic ash had accumulated during the past autumn, I was usually able to find scores of the little worms as lively and happy as refrigerated worms could possibly be. Here they live and breed and rear their young in what appears to be a perfectly normal (for glacier worms) fashion. I cannot conceive of even an earthworm living healthfully on nothing but volcanic ash and pumice, so there must be something else to nourish them. This something no doubt is the abundant microscopic plant life, such as the "red snow" we saw in Paradise Valley, which also lives in the old snow and ice of the glacier. There is also a certain amount of vegetable and animal matter carried up by the wind from timberline. We often saw pipits and rosy finches feeding on the icefields and discovered that they were picking up insects and seeds that had been carried there by the strong south winds. In Grasshopper Glacier, in the northeast corner of Yellowstone National Park, there are imbedded layers of grasshoppers or locusts that were carried there hundreds of years ago by the wind, or perhaps a migrating swarm was caught in a snowstorm and forced down and buried, just as airplanes have been so caught in more recent times. There are also several species of insects mostly of the lowly order of Thysanura or springtails that are regular inhabitants of glaciers.

A point of rock, a veritable "steamboat prow," separates the Stevens and the Paradise lobes of the glacier and here we always stopped to rest and to admire the view. This rock is called Marmot Point and it not only overlooks the mile-deep canyon of Stevens Creek and the Cowlitz River but the entire mass of the Cascades to the south. Bulky Mount Adams and graceful Mount St. Helens look very close, and between the two stands Mount Hood beyond the Columbia River in Oregon. On clear days Mount Jefferson some fifty miles farther south can also be seen.

Within sound of Marmot Rock is Sluiskin Falls at the head of Paradise Valley, but it is out of sight below the rim.

11

DURING THIS REST I USUALLY TOLD the people something of the geology of Mount Rainier upon whose shoulder we perched, and related the thrilling account of the first attempts to climb to its summit. From here we could trace the summit route all the way to the top.

On the skyline a few miles to our left we could see the tumbled ice of the Kautz Glacier, which was named for (then) Lieutenant A. V. Kautz, an officer of the United States Army. In the summer of 1857, when Lieutenant Kautz was stationed at Fort Steilacoom near the mouth of the Nisqually River on Puget Sound, he and three soldiers made the first attempt to reach the summit. This was in mid-July but the weather was bad and the party ill equipped. With an old Nisqually brave named Wapowety as a guide, the party scrambled through the trailless jungles as far as the terminus of the Nisqually Glacier. Then stopped by stormy weather, they climbed over the left moraine and made camp in Van Trump Park at about the same elevation as Marmot Rock. Kautz was a good soldier—he later became a general—but he was no naturalist. At this camp he saw strange animals grazing in the meadows. When disturbed these animals gave a shrill warning whistle and disappeared into the mountainside. Kautz, like a good soldier, investigated cautiously. He found large burrows in the ground and in the loose dirt at their entrance were the tracks of a cloven-hoofed animal. Later he wrote a thrilling account of the expedition which was quite accurate in most respects but it did describe "lamb-like animals which lived in burrows on the mountain." This was too much for naturalists to accept and Kautz remained a very puzzled man.

Of course the Lieutenant's "grazing whistlers" were the big hoary marmots of Mount Rainier and there was a family of them living in a burrow just under where we sat. The tracks were made by the mountain goats which still live in Van Trump Park, where I was often able to point them out to my parties on the Nisqually Glacier trip.

The next day Kautz, three soldiers, and the Indian started for the summit, which appeared to be only a few hours' climb away. By early afternoon they were still a long way from the summit and one of the soldiers returned to camp with Wapowety, who was suffering from snow blindness. Soon the second soldier, who was grossly overweight, lagged behind and only Kautz and one soldier were left. They finally reached an elevation of about fourteen thousand feet and were there stopped by icefalls and crevasses. The soldier refused to go on and Lieutenant Kautz soon gave up also. It was, as he wrote, "what may be called the top, for although there were points higher yet, the mountain spread out comparatively flat. . . . "

Summit and crater of Mount Rainier from about 20,000 feet. The elevation at the summit is 14,410 feet. Steam jets about the edges of the crater keep the rim bare of snow and form caverns under the snow where climbers can take shelter. Camp Comfort is the rock at bottom center. (Photo by National Park Service)

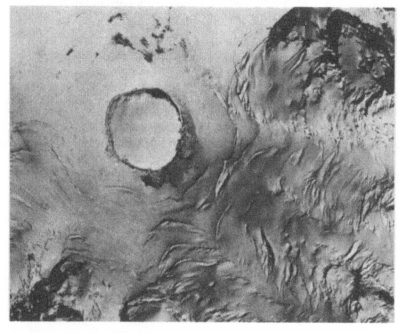

Poorly equipped and inexperienced as they were, it was a valiant effort and Kautz Glacier with Wapowety Cleaver beyond justly honor the two leaders of the expedition.

It was thirteen years later before another attempt, this time successful, was made on the old mountain. It was mid-August of 1870 when General Hazard Stevens and P. V. Van Trump, with a Cowlitz Indian named Sluiskin as a guide, made a final camp at the edge of the meadow just a hundred yards from where we sat. Hazard Stevens was the son of the first governor of Washington Territory, and served in the Civil War as an officer on his father's staff. The father was killed while leading the charge at Chantilly and the son was severely wounded. He was mustered out at the end of the war as a brigadier general of volunteers and returned to Washington Territory, where he took up farming near Olympia. His neighbor, Van Trump, was an experienced mountaineer. (Van Trump made a second ascent in 1883 with James Longmire, and at the time to which I am referring he was still living, and telling the story of his adventures at every opportunity. Until only five years before this time, he had been a National Park Ranger living at Indian Henry's Ranger Station.)

Sluiskin, who had actually never been so far up the mountain before, refused to take any responsibility beyond the snow line, and he warned Stevens and Van Trump that "there are demons who dwell in a lake of fire at the summit and no one can make the ascent and live. If you should escape the perils of rock and ice," he told them, "and reach the great snowy dome a bitterly cold and furious tempest will sweep you off into space like a withered leaf, and if by some miracle you should survive all these perils, the mighty demon of Tahoma will surely throw you into the fiery lake. Don't go," he urged them.

In spite of Sluiskin's pessimism the two pushed on, but only after Sluiskin had demanded and received a "signed paper" absolving him from all blame for their death.

Equipped with crampons and ice axes and skilled in climbing, the two reached the summit after eleven grueling hours. It was then so late that they were forced to spend the night in a steam cave which they discovered under the snow within the summit crater. When they returned safely to camp near the end of the second day they found Sluiskin just packing to leave the mountain with the story of their death. He was very happy to see them nevertheless, and feasted them on broiled marmot, four of which he had taken from the vicinity of Marmot Rock and prepared as food for his return trip.

On our way down Mazama Ridge and back to the inn we would usually pause again at the foot of Sluiskin Falls to admire the view and to watch the family of water ouzels that always nested there.

12

I HAD ONE WORRISOME EXPERIENCE on Stevens Glacier that summer due to fog. Clouds often blow in from the Pacific at about eight thousand feet elevation and strike the mountain just above timberline. These may be seen from below as just scattered cumulus clouds in a clear sky, but when they strike the mountain they are a dense fog.

My party started out in the sunlight and was in the middle of the glacier when we were suddenly blanketed by one of these clouds. The only landmark was the contour of the snow field. I knew of course that I had to go downhill. But there are two lobes of the Stevens Glacier split by Marmot Rock. If I came out only a few feet to the left of Marmot Rock I would come to the snout of the Stevens lobe which is lower than the Paradise, and the headwall of impassable Stevens Canyon. To the right of Marmot Rock I would strike the trail on Mazama Ridge alongside the Paradise lobe of the glacier. This is what I had to find after a mile's traverse of the snow fields. We could not see ten yards, and the total lack of shadows made walking hazardous on the uneven snow. Several times I stumbled into depressions that I could not see in front of me. I was worried and the people knew it, so I asked them to hold onto the rope and told them we would move very slowly. I assured them that we would soon get below the fog.

Everyone was calm except one redhead who became more and more hysterical as time went on. Every few minutes she would call out, "Guide, are you lost?" We were going downhill more steeply than we should. To turn back would have been the safest thing to do, but it would have been an admission that I was lost. I was afraid this woman would start screeching any minute. So I kept bearing to the right and tried to hold my elevation. After a time I came to a very steep slope and had to ask the party to wait while I went ahead to reconnoiter. This proved to the party that I was lost, but I soon saw that we were at the tip of the Stevens terminus and then I knew where I had to go. We had to go back, but we quickly climbed up to Marmot Rock and the trail. We were an hour overdue by now and I knew that the guidehouse would be worried, but I had to stop to let the party rest.

My redheaded worry-bird collapsed on the ground and hugged the rock, but she relieved tensions all around by jumping up in a moment and calling out: "Guide I can't wait another minute. Keep everyone right here. I'm going down the trail." And as she disappeared in the fog she called back: "Now you all stay right there, I won't be a minute."

We had not gone far down the trail when we met Hans and the guide manager coming up with ropes and first-aid kits. I knew they were looking for us, but they saw at a glance that we were all right, so passed on after a moment's chat about the weather, saying that they were going out to explore new ice caverns.

They were back at the guidehouse, however, when I checked in after having delivered my party at the inn in time for a late supper.

13

THE TRIP WHICH I ENJOYED MOST that summer was the Pinnacle Peak climb. I have climbed Pinnacle many times since and I still enjoy it. Pinnacle, although not the highest, is the dominant peak of the Tatoosh Range which lies south of the great mass of the mountain. "Tatoosh" is also the name of an island off the northwest tip of the Olympic Peninsula. It is said to be an Indian word meaning "nourishing breast." This range is of older stuff than the Johnny-come-lately volcanic cone which looks down upon it—a saw-toothed basaltic spur of the Cascade Mountains which stand some fifteen miles to the east. Pinnacle rises three thousand feet above the canyon floor and almost in the middle of the range.

I recall one of my earlier climbs in some detail. It was not my first ascent. The first I made alone after supper one evening in early July. I found my way from instructions given me by Wes Langlow, another of the guides, and from following scratches made by climbing boots on the rock. Actually there is only one feasible route to the summit of Pinnacle and it is not difficult to find it by a process of elimination. I ran most of the way and was home by dark.

The second trip I made as a member of a climbing party led by Heinie. After that I led parties myself.

On this trip I had five climbers. Leaving Paradise Valley and going down to the river, the trail was easy although it was muddy in spots from melting snow, and cut up some by the horses. Devil's Dip with the snow gone is only a series of short switchbacks. We crossed the river on a foot log. When we came back in the evening, water would be breaking over the log so I would tie up a hand rope, but the foot log was dry this morning and safe. I helped the women off the high end.

At the top of Mazama Ridge there is a small marshy meadow with a tiny lake which reflects the mountain. Cotton grass, marsh marigolds, buttercup, and shooting stars grow there and we stopped to rest. There were water lilies, the yellow so-called American lotus, and green frogs in the pond.

Around Reflection Lake a half-mile farther on were fields of big multiflowered avalanche lilies, and the anemone were opening but the heather was not yet in bloom.

Beyond Reflection Lake we climbed a steep track down which water ran from the melting snow. The area is subalpine, with dwarf firs, cedars, and tangles of huckleberry bushes. There are mountain ash and white rhododendron also. Here and there are islands of larger trees, alpine firs and mountain hemlocks that have, on exposed ridges and outcroppings, avoided the avalanches and some of the snow, found a longer growing season, and finally succeeded in growing above the late-lying snowdrifts that stunt and break the smaller trees. This is a north slope and snow lies until midsummer. At places the trail is so steep that we pulled ourselves up by the bushes and in other places we clambered up the bed of Pinnacle Creek between boulders and over slippery ledges.

Within an hour we were on the snow-covered talus slopes below the glacier and soon on the ice field itself. Pinnacle Glacier is a typical cirque glacier, lying in a bowl-shaped depression (with one side out) which it has gouged for itself in the face of the range, so that the lower slopes—the bottom of the bowl—are gentle. It was a relief to walk upright for a few hundred yards across this depression. Later in the year because of melting snow there would be a snow lake here.

It took a half-hour of slow climbing to kick our way up the last five hundred feet to the Saddle. Here we rested again and admired the view. We could see Paradise Inn and cars creeping up the narrow ribbon which is the highway, far below us.

It was now after eleven. I wanted to have lunch on the summit.

You can walk almost horizontally across the back face of Pinnacle. The wall appears unclimbable on the right, and the slope below, although loose rock and mountain meadow, appears so steep that once a person started rolling he would not stop for a mile. It is best to watch the trail ahead. After a couple hundred yards of this we came to a small clump of dwarf trees where we could stop and study our final ascent.

"We go up from here," I told them. "We will go slowly. I will carry the rope and the ladies' lunchboxes in my pack. We will leave your alpenstocks and my ice ax here and pick them up on the way down. Watch where I go. Try every step and handhold before you throw your weight on it. If any rock falls, call out. Keep close together. If anyone feels at all faint at any time let me know immediately.

One of the girls asked, as someone always did, "I can see how we can get up, but how can we get down?" I told them not to worry about that, that actually it was much easier than it looked, and that I wouldn't leave anyone on the top.

It is like climbing a ladder, and almost as steep, but moving cautiously and slowly we were on top within an hour.

There are a few low, white-barked pines on the summit of Pinnacle, and some dwarfed Alaska cedars. Gray jays come up when climbers are in sight and they, and a few chipmunks, are quite willing to share the raisins and nuts from the box lunches put up by the inn. These chipmunks interest me. Are they summer residents who come up only because of climbers' lunches, or do they live all year around on this arctic spire? And how did they get up there in the first place?

I have never seen marmots or conies on top, but there are colonies of them in the rock slides all around the base of the peak, and we could hear their calls from far below; the frequent nasal "echs" of the cony and the occasional shrill whistle of the marmot. We had seen the little haycocks of the conies on the way up.

We had no trouble getting down and soon stood in the Saddle at the top of Pinnacle Glacier. This is the big thrill for most people, something to be remembered longer even than the tremendous view from the summit. I explained how to slide. "Just sit loose. Let nature take its course. But don't roll, you might get hurt. If you start rolling flatten out on the snow, spread-eagle, and the snow will stop you. Now watch me . . . I'll go first." I then shoved off, dragging all the alpenstocks behind me and was down in a minute or two. I waved and called for the rest to come one at a time. They came screaming and yelling, every which way, all over the place, but no one was hurt. Some people always want to climb back up and do it over again but there is seldom time. We barely got home in time for supper.

14

I WAS ENJOYING MY GUIDE WORK and learning to love the old mountain more and more. Climbing grows on one, an indefinable sort of wanderlust which gets in the blood and makes one restless and curious to see "the other side of the mountain." This led to my next adventure.

We were sitting in the equipment room of the guidehouse one evening working on gear and clothing. There was always plenty to do in what spare time we had and it was a good place to talk. Heinie was showing me how to put edging nails on climbing boots. Wes and some of the boys were tinning pants. "Tin pants" are a local product worn on the Stevens Glacier trip for "nature coasting." The boys were smearing hot paraffin on the seats of duck trousers and ironing it in with an electric iron. The paraffin is not for lubrication—you don't need that—but it does help to keep the wearer dry.

But Wes and the boys were not talking about tin pants or nature coasting. They were discussing a ragged, three-fingered peak in the Tatoosh Range which we could see from the guidehouse windows. This peak had no name, and according to Wes it had never been climbed. The U.S.G.S. topographic map hanging on the guidehouse wall gave its elevation as six thousand feet and it did not appear, either from the map or from the window, any more difficult to scale than several of its sister peaks. Pinnacle Peak, 6,562 feet and second to the east, is the most spectacular—a little Matterhorn. Unicorn, four peaks to the east, is the highest in the range (6,939 feet), the most difficult and most dangerous to climb, but even it had been scaled a number of times.

Wes was explaining that the first party to make an ascent of a virgin peak thereby earns the right to give it a name, and he was proposing that the three of them scale this peak on their first free half-day and that they then christen it "The Three Gentlemen" because of its three summits and its three conquistadors. I had a half-day off the very next day and I secretly decided that I would beat Wes and the boys to the climb.

I told Ruth my plans, and although she was not happy about me climbing alone, she did not object. She could watch me with field glasses from our camp during the first and last stages of the climb. Had it not been for the baby I would have taken her along.

I took the trail to Reflection Lake, then climbed directly up Pinnacle Creek to Pinnacle Glacier. The ice of Pinnacle Glacier was still covered with snow and I had no trouble kicking steps all the way up to the saddle. Ruth followed me quite easily that far, since the distance is not much more than three miles in an air line.

From the saddle I worked my way across the back (south) face of Pinnacle—the north face is a sheer rock wall—and came out again in the saddle between Pinnacle and Plummer Peaks. Here below Plummer Peak I found one of the most exquisite little alpine parks I have ever seen. It lies in a cirque surrounded by tall spires of dark basalt and in the middle is a tiny lake or tarn. This day it was still half-filled with the snow of a tardy snowbank, but around the pool and the snowbank were acres of mountain flowers nodding in a light breeze—a fabulous display of nature's artistry. So far as I know the little lake, or the park in which it lies, has no name and is still untouched in any way by the hand of man. Only a relatively few fortunate souls have ever seen it.

I crossed this meadow to the foot of the unnamed peak and examined the south face for a possible route to the summit. There were two fairly safe-appearing routes, two "chimneys," one between each pair of the trident points of the summit. I chose the east, or right-hand chimney, and started up.

It was easy climbing, hard rock with plenty of good foot and hand holds, and within an hour I was on the east summit. I rested there for a bit and waved my shirt in case Ruth was still following me with the glasses.

Then I climbed down into the high saddle and up again to the highest rock of the central spire. It was now late afternoon and the view was breathtaking. The great dome of Rainier filled the sky to the north and, with the four-thousand-foot-deep Nisqually Canyon at my feet, the mountain appeared bigger and higher than I had ever seen it before. Forty miles to the south the Fuji-like cone of Mount St. Helens stood chalk-white in the afternoon light. Farther to the southeast stood bulky Mount Adams, and between the two, more than a hundred miles away and beyond the Columbia River in Oregon, sat stately Mount Hood. Nearby on either hand ranged the rocky spires of the Tatoosh, and almost below me to the south lay the tiny lake in its setting of spring flowers, their gayness dimmed now and blended by the long dark shadows cast by the surrounding peaks.

While I sat resting and enjoying the view I was suddenly startled by a swish and a shadow, and I ducked just as a huge bird, yellow talons outstretched, flashed past my right shoulder. It was an eagle, and I am convinced it tried to strike me. Only the slight sound of wings, or a premonition of danger, saved my life.

At the moment I thought the eagle must have a nest nearby and was trying to frighten me away from her eggs or young, just as crows, or even hummingbirds, have often tried to do. Although I searched carefully, I could see no sign of a nest, and the eagle did not return to the attack. Later I learned that there are known instances of eagles striking large animals, such as mountain goat, when they find them at the brink of a precipice, thereby knocking off and killing larger game than they could hope to kill in a normal encounter. I think now that this eagle mistook me for a goat. I was glad that he found out differently.

When I looked around for evidence of other climbers I soon found a small rock cairn and in it a Prince Albert tobacco tin. In the tin was a page from a pocket notebook bearing the three names of a Tacoma climbing party dated the previous August. I added my name and the date to the sheet, replaced the can, and climbed quickly down to the base of the peak. It was now near sunset, and my still nameless peak cast a long dark shadow across the landscape. Again I sat for a moment, resting and drinking in the calm and peaceful atmosphere of the Alpine scene.

On the talus slope nearby round-eared conies were also enjoying the evening calm after a hard day of haying; and a fat marmot, less provident than the conies, was nibbling at the new leaves of the purple lupine by the lake.

I was sitting, I discovered, on the lip of a goat bed with my feet in the dry volcanic ash. In such places, like the buffalo wallows of the plains, the white mountain goats lie and kick dust over themselves to discourage the flies. These beds are used year after year and become so deep that I have seen goats lying in them with only their heads sticking out as though they were peering from the entrance of a cave they had excavated into the hillside. This day I saw no goat but their fresh droppings and square-toed tracks were all about the meadow. Deer tracks, which I also saw, are sharp-toed, and the track of the bighorn sheep are much larger.

When I looked down at my feet my eye was caught by what appeared to be a fragment of glass and I reached down idly and picked it up. It was the upper half of an Indian arrowhead and it was of glass, or rather a transparent obsidian, a form of volcanic glass. It was beautifully chipped and I knew that it must have come from the Columbia Basin region beyond the Cascades—the weapon probably of a Yakima hunter, or of a Cowlitz tribesman who had secured it by barter from his Yakima cousins. So far as I can learn this is the only arrowpoint ever found on the mountain, or as near to it as the Tatoosh Range. This scarcity of artifacts gives weight to the stories that the Indians never lived on the mountain and seldom hunted there, but whether it was from fear of the gods who dwelt in Tahoma's fire pit, as the legends say, or from the sheer fact of inaccessibility, I am not certain.

No mountain sheep exist on the mountain today and the nearest bands are to be found three hundred miles to the southeast in the Wallowa Mountains of Oregon or a similar distance to the northeast in the Selkirks of Canada. Ben Longmire's story of finding a set of big ram's horns while building trail at the foot of the Tatoosh is the only fairly authentic story I have of bighorn sheep ever inhabiting the central Cascades, although most of it is ideal sheep country.

15

I REMEMBERED BEN'S STORY AND WONDERED—could this arrow have killed the last of the bighorns on Mount Rainier? I held it in my hand and in my imagination I saw a great ram standing at the edge of the cliff and silhouetted against the northern sky. Below in that clump of fir trees crouched the Cowlitz hunter, bow drawn. All around stood the black basaltic peaks. Not a sound was anywhere to be heard.

It was Kenya, last of the bighorn sheep, and he was doomed. Neither he, nor the Indian, nor the gods of the mountain above could do anything now to save him.

For Kenya it had all started right here in this meadow, and with him it would all end. He had been born in Tatoosh Park, this park, one of twin lambs. There was a small band then; his mother the old ewe who led the flock, the ancient ram who was his father, and a half-dozen younger ewes

Last of the bighorns

and yearling rams who ran with his mother and avoided the belligerent old ram who was their father also. Kenya and his twin sister were the only lambs born to the flock that season.

And now he was the last of the band. Indian hunters to the south, cougar in the forest they had crossed, the eagle which had carried off his little sister, and the slow attrition of the years had combined to take all the others and leave him alone.

For more than a year now he had been a desolate wanderer—across the Muddy Fork, up the Packwood, over the Goat Rocks and down to the Cispus, then across the cinder slopes of Mount Adams, past Walupt Lake, down through the dark forests to Mount St. Helens, back to the raging Cispus and up the Muddy Fork to the Tatoosh again—a hundred rugged miles of rock and ice, forest and swamp, and now back to the alpine meadows, and not once in all this time and space had he seen another of his kind or crossed the trail of another mountain sheep. There were shaggy white goats in the high country, huge elk in the forests, and black-tailed deer in the parks and meadows, but all these he ignored. There were cougar and bobcat and bear, and there were Indians also, and these he avoided.

But an Indian had seen him on Mount Adams, a young buck who had loitered along the ridges while the women and young girls gathered blueberries on the slopes below and the old men slept and smoked in their camp by the lake where they minded the ponies and the babies. This young buck dreamed he was a great hunter and he boasted in the camp that night that he would follow the great ram and kill him. Before them all he had boasted and now he must make good his boast.

He planned his campaign well. If it took weeks he would take weeks. If it led him to the very slopes of Tahoma he would go. He would defy the gods of the mountain. He had sworn to bring back the head of the big-horn ram—before the old men he had sworn it and a man does not swear oaths lightly.

Kenya had seen the hunter's approach a day's journey away but he had refused to leave the ranges. For a week he had avoided the hunter in the high rocks. Always the Indian kept below him to cut off his retreat. In all this time neither man nor ram had rested and neither had eaten very much. Finally the Indian had tried another tactic. He had hidden himself at night in this clump of firs and had waited silently. Sooner or later the big ram must come down to the meadow to feed and to drink.

Now he had come.

One sharp whistle of a marmot, one screech of a jay, one snap of a twig or rattle of a stone might have warned him; but no marmot whistled, no jay screeched, and no twig snapped. The morning was still as death itself and the arrow flew silently.

Kenya leaped too late. The shaft passed through his massive neck, a mortal wound. He stumbled and fell, then with an effort regained his feet. Now the Indian was rushing up the slope toward him, fitting another arrow to the bowstring as he ran. But this arrow was never loosed. With his last strength Kenya leaped out and down—down, down, to the rocks below.

The Cowlitz hunter fell on his belly and peered over. Far below on the talus slope he saw the broken body of the great ram. The cliff was unclimbable. Not even a mountain goat could have scaled it. The Indian looked to the right and to the left. On each side the rocks rose sheer, unbroken. Then he stood up and raised his eyes. There before him towered the great mountain—Tahoma, the dwelling place of the gods. For days he had been near it but always in the shadow of the lesser peaks. Not once had he seen it. Now it loomed above him; it almost leaned over him. He was startled and he was frightened. He had displeased the gods. He had killed the last of the bighorn sheep. He reached for his medicine pouch at his belt. He would ask forgiveness of the great spirit. He would appease the wrath of the mountain gods.

But the pouch was gone. Somewhere he had lost it. His gods had forsaken him. The mountain bore down on him. He started to raise his arms in supplication, and then he turned and fled down the mountainside.

Fiction, pure fiction, but the time and the place were right for dreaming.

I barely had time to slide down the Pinnacle Glacier and make my way through the mountain ash and boulders along Pinnacle Creek before darkness overtook me. When I reached the trail at Reflection Lake it was entirely dark. But soon the moon came over Mazama Ridge and I had no trouble following the trail back to Paradise Valley. Ruth was waiting up and badly worried when I arrived. I showed her the arrowhead, which I still have.

Next morning at the guidehouse I said nothing about my adventures, and the following day Wes and the two junior guides made their ascent of the unnamed peak. They gave me some quizzical looks

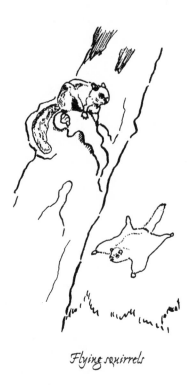

Flying squirrels

when they returned but they made no public announcements either and the peak remained unnamed, if not unclimbed, until several years later when the National Park Service officially named it Lane Peak in honor of Franklin K. Lane, Secretary of the Interior, who was then retiring after many years of meritorious service. I have never climbed it since.

16

SO SPRING FLOWED INTO SUMMER as unobtrusively as morning into afternoon. The days remained long and bright, the weather mild, and the tourists began to spread like a colony of ants over the base of a gigantic anthill. The mountain stood serenely aloft, little concerned with the rustlings in her skirts. She reigned over a bigger, broader world.

Still there were powers over which even a mountain cannot rule. In time the sun would melt her mantle of ice and the released water, drawn irresistibly downward by the gravitational pull of the earth and aided and abetted by the wind, would slowly change the contours of her face, for even the "eternal" mountains have within them the forces of their own destruction and although spasmodic convulsions may toss them high, the long slow processes of nature will always bring them low again and some-day even Mount Rainier will be a rolling plain.

But in mid-July reluctant snowbanks still lurked behind dense clumps of alpine firs on the north slopes of Alta Vista and lay deep on the lower side of the inn, although the hillside above the hotel was entirely free of snow and the silvery pompoms which are the seed pods of the Western anemone sat like troops of little gray monkeys in the grass. The tobacco-shaped leaves and corn-tassel panicles of the green-flowered false helle-bore stood four or five feet high in the flower fields and dominated the ranks of blue lupine, wild parsnip, mountain dock, and Sitka valerian. Here and there on the crest of the ridges were rounded tussocks of Indian basket grass, like the shakos of careless bandmasters left lying on the drill field. Soon these would bear tall plumes as white as snow and more beau-tiful than tassels of feather or fur. Local Indians prize the tough grasslike leaves of this distant cousin of the lilies which is also called "bear grass," and travel each year into the high meadows to gather it for their basket making.

But the real and visible evidence that spring was past and summer had arrived was the blooming of the heather. Entire hillsides blushed with the purple bloom, and on the exposed summits of the lesser hills the deep-green mats of bride's heather were stringing their dainty white bells. Learned botanists, more technically minded than I, refer to these two choice flowers as the red mountain heath *(Phyllodoce empetriformis)* and Merten's Cassiope *(Cassiope mertensiana),* but they look like the "bonny, bonny heather" of Scotland, and the rare highland bride's heather to me; and whoever (besides Homer, Virgil, and a botany professor) ever heard of Phyllodoce and Cassiope?

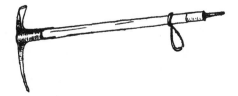

summer

GIBRALTAR ROUTE

1. The Guide House
2. Alta Vista
3. Glacier Rim
4. Timberline
5. Panorama Point
6. McClure Rock
7. Camp Muir
8. The Beehive

9. Camp Misery
10. The Chutes
11. Camp Comfort
12. Crater Rim
13. Gibraltar Rock
14. Little Tahoma
15. Anvil Rock

1

IT IS SUMMER, THE FRUITFUL SEASON of the year, which finds the mountain meadows at their mellow best. There are cynics among Park Service employees who because of their duties must be year-round residents of the high country. They are wont to say: "We have no summer up here really, . . . only about ten months of winter and two of late fall," and it is true that snow often falls at some time during every month of a year. But in spite of this, summer *is,* and no matter how brief it may be, it is a happy, busy, lovely season. It is summer, no matter what the weather is like, when trees and lesser flowering plants hug tight the fleeting warmth of air and earth and strain every fiber and tissue to mature and deliver their precious brood. Ruth and I knew it was summer because this same bewitching process was going on within our own little family, within the families of the ground squirrels who lived and fought domestically beneath our tent floor and the noisy woodpeckers nesting in the hollow trees behind our camp.

The old mountain herself is a motherly matron of a mountain. Long since she has lost the seductive curves and firm clean lines of her younger sister, Mount St. Helens, but neither is she old and broken-down like Mount Hood or Mount Shasta who, although they wear well the dignity and grace of age, are long past their productive prime. The lines carved into her rugged face by the abrasive tools of time give strength and dignity rather than a look of decadence or senility. She is a proud vigorous old girl, through with the flash and frivolity of youth but far from the stuffy complacency of a resigned middle age. Although called dormant by volcanologists, her pulse is still hot and strong. She may still have the capacity for violence and it is not impossible that some whim of her nature may yet assert itself in a last great volcanic fling. Frequent internal rumblings and earthquake shocks give notice that the hot breaths of her summit crater are not mere residual vapors but rise from large molten masses still lying deep within her ample frame. A last bold assertion of her receding youth, such as the Mount Katmai eruptions of 1912 or the Mount Lassen rampages a few years later, would provide a magnificent show for residents of the Northwest and, since volcanoes usually give warning of their violent intents, would likely do no irreparable damage to human habitations, there being no cities close enough to be buried like Pompeii or Herculaneum at the foot of Vesuvius. The gravest danger would be from floods caused by rapidly melting snow and ice in contact with incandescent gasses, cinder, or even molten lava. But it is to be hoped that the good lady will be content to grow old gracefully as ladies should, for a violent eruption would destroy all the delicate loveliness of ice stream and snow field, alpine meadow and flower-filled valley, and leave only a black cinder cone and fire-scarred forests such as were left around Katmai and Lassen.

It is this delicate summer dress of crystal snow, flowing water, and fresh green growing things which sets her off to perfection.

Mount Rainier has a history vastly longer than that of its human observers. Although young, geologically speaking, the mountain can still boast a respectable age. Along with its sister volcanoes, which are scattered like a rim of fire clear around the forty-thousand-mile circumference of the Western ocean, Rainier made geological history. For a hundred thousand years, perhaps, it dominated a scene of violent upheaval. During this time its fires were one of the colossal earth-building agencies which with explosive eruptions and lava flows built the continents and crowded the oceans into their present basins.

The warping and wrinkling of the cooling planet pushed up the north-south ranges (of which the Sierra Nevada and Cascades were then the most recent) and fractured the basement strata so that the residual heat still trapped below the congealing surface rocks built up pressures too great to be contained. These broke out at the weaker spots into roaring volcanoes.

Rainier was one of the greatest of these fire mountains, although the one hundred or more cubic miles of material which was spewed out its open crater was a trivial amount compared with the vast mass of the Columbia basalt which, at about the same time, boiled up through hidden fissures and spread out up to four thousand feet deep over half the states of Washington and Oregon and part of Idaho—a once molten lake of lava larger than all of New England.

Ancestors of the Ice Age mammoths and mastodons, or even the last remaining bands of America's prehorses, may have been witnesses to this earth-rending inferno, and many of them no doubt were victims of its fires, but it is not likely that any human beings viewed the scene. Man came later—after the earth had cooled, the Columbia Basin lava had been covered with grasslands, and the cinder and lava cones clothed in forests. Some of the earliest human immigrants from Asia may have shivered through the following ice ages which drove all life southward, and their descendants may have been the bold pioneers who followed the retreating glaciers northward again and repopulated the forests and grasslands which had already clothed the gutted valleys.

Mount Rainier, and the other volcanoes to the north and south, were submerged during these thousands of years of winter, and their mantles of ice merged into the vast glacier which was pushing southward along the lower valleys. But the ice above had no influence upon the fires within, and the old volcanoes went on with their business of building a new earth.

Recently, except for Lassen Peak some four hundred miles to the south, these volcanoes have become quiescent. They still smolder inside, but for most of them their violent days are over and their last feeble efforts to regain their old fire have resulted in only minor explosions and rumblings. Now in their decadence the forces of erosion have gained the upper hand, and the icy fingers of the remaining glaciers are tearing them down faster than they will ever be able to build themselves up again. Rainier, as is the fate of mountains as well as men, is being slowly returned to the great mass of mother earth which bore it. Still it proudly carries its snow-filled crater (from which now only whiffs of steam drift upward), some 14,410 feet above the level of Puget Sound which lies in the glacier-cut trough at its feet; and many more generations of Indians, along with their pale-faced brothers, will be able to gather blueberries on its parklike ridges and in its flower-filled meadows.

2

INDIANS STILL COME EACH SUMMER to camp in the high mountain meadows and gather blueberries for their winter larder. These are Yakima from east of the Cascade summit, or Cowlitz from the remnant of that tribe still living along the lower Columbia. A few come on foot, leading pack ponies heavily loaded with their gear, but mostly these days they come by car. The car may be the latest model, but the men and women are still people of the "old days." The men have long hair worn in two

Blueberries

ropelike braids tied with a bit of red cloth, and the women wear deerskin moccasins. Among their berrying equipment may still be found ancient baskets woven of cedar roots and tight enough to hold water. At the camp at Fairy Lake one day I tried to buy such a basket, half-full of fat blueberries with the bloom still on them, but the old grandmother who owned it was not interested in selling. Such baskets are rare today even among the Indians.

While the women and children gather berries the old men sit in camp, tending the babies and looking at the mountain. They seldom exhibit any interest in exploring the glaciers or climbing the peaks. So far as I know the Indians have never ventured above timberline. An Indian, fully at home on his woodland trails, would be ill equipped to climb over the broken lava and ice of the upper reaches shod only in deerskin moccasins.

But of greater significance to the Indians is the fact that this is "Tahoma," *The Mountain,* and they have long held its upper slopes in awe. For within the memory of men still living, earthquakes have rocked the mountain, causing great avalanches of stone and ice. Naturally they attribute these phenomena to the spirits who dwell at the summit, and the Indians want no truck with gods capable of such violence.

3

As SUMMER ADVANCED, A GRAYNESS appeared in the tips of the tall blue-green alpine firs beside our tent. On close inspection it turned out to be a dense mass of small cones, part of a fascinating reproductive process.

Cones hang *below* the twigs on most conifers, but in a few species they sit upright on the branches like sleepy little owls. This is most noticeable on the true cedars, *atlantica, libani,* and *deodara,* where the cones are almost as big as owls and grow at random all over the trees. On the balsam firs, cones are borne only on the topmost branches, and there they sit like a whole flock of owls.

Trees, like all flowering and seed-producing plants, have highly complex sexual arrangements, no different, except in minor details, from those of the animals, including man. A so-called "perfect" flower, such as an apple blossom, has both male and female sex organs side by side in the same flower. Incest is not the custom, however, as sexual union does not ordinarily take place between brother and sister apple blossoms. Since social pressures do not operate among plants this law is enforced by a careful timing of the sexual maturity of the different parts of the flowers, making self-pollination improbable and cross-pollination likely.

In other species, such as the oaks and the pines, the sex organs—the male and the female flowers, or if you wish to be technical, the staminate and the pistillate flowers—are born separate but on the same tree. In this case the tree, or other plant, is called monoecious—as opposed to dioecious plants like the cottonwood and holly, whose flowers are born separate and on separate trees.

The alpine firs beside our tent were monoecious. In early spring little scaly cylinders form under the upper branches from buds of the previous year. They are the male or pollen-bearing flowers. A little later, conelike female flowers appear sitting erect on the upperside of the terminal branches. When these strobiles are impregnated by wind-blown pollen from other fir trees and conception takes place, the fertile cone develops rapidly and matures its seed in one season. (Most cone-bearing trees require two seasons.) By late fall the cones of the alpine fir are about three inches long, slim, and purple-gray. From a distance they appear to be black.

Then another unusual thing happens. Pine cones mature, dry out, expand, and open their scales, allowing the winged seeds to fall out from their cozy, fur-lined, prenatal cavities, and wing away over the hills like little helicopters. Later the dead cones fall from the tree. The fir cones, however, never fall off. The cone scales fall, releasing the seeds, and only the conical core of the cone remains on the tree. In late fall and winter these spikes look like rows of black candies on the branches of a Christmas tree. In midsummer, however, the cones were covered by a blue-gray bloom, half-formed, and as beautiful as a maiden in the first blush of womanhood.

This preoccupation with reproduction on the part of the plants has always interested me, and never more so than the summer we were awaiting our first child. All the vast energy of the growing organism is channeled in this one direction. The roots tolerate no obstruction in their constant search for food and moisture; the stems struggle heroically to lift the leaves to their place in the sun; the leaves are the busiest of factories combining the numerous elements, with the energy from the sun and under the guidance of the green slavemaster chlorophyll, into complex starches and sugars with which to build more roots, more stem, and more leaves. But never for a moment are the roots, stems, and leaves the final objective. They are only the necessary means to the end. The objective is always the seed. If there is a surplus of food stored in any part of the plant it is only that more and better seed can be produced. If there are showy flowers it is only that there may be a greater certainty of seed. If there is abundant and tasty fruit it is only because fruit is the mother of the seed borne within it. Seed is the assurance of new life, and new life is the reason for living.

So reproduction becomes the total occupation of the plant. If in its abundant growth it feeds all the vast array of animals on the earth (for animals, who can manufacture no basic food for themselves, are in a sense parasitic upon plants); if in growing, it clothes the continents in verdure and gives rest and shade to man; if it controls floods, prevents erosion, modifies climate, houses a swarm of bees or a nest of birds; if it heals the body, pleases the eye, and inspires to song—all these things are incidental, unimportant, trivial. The plant lives for none of these things. The plant lives to procreate its kind. Procreation is its expectation of immortality. Death is the deadline for the individual, but there is no deadline for the race. Death for the plant is accepted, but death for the race of plants is never accepted. For the race of plants death is avoidable and to be avoided.

No plant or animal believes in a second chance, an afterworld. "Heaven" is a concept for fearful men. To the plant there is no end to this world. In a very real sense each individual plant lives on in its descendants. Each seed or spore is a tiny, highly potent bundle of life. With its germination and growth the plant in effect gets a new lease on life, catches its breath, gets its "second wind." In reality life has not ceased. The parent plant, tired from the struggle, merely passes the ball on to a new carrier.

This is *procreation,* but *creation* is something more than reproduction. If the life passed on has been enriched, expanded, glorified, then *procreation* becomes *creation*. Creation hints strongly of immortality and eternity.

The Hindu concept of reincarnation recognizes this need for unending, continual creation. When the soul lives again in a new life it is always hoped that this new life will be on a higher level of existence, and for one to fail in the present life endangers this hope for a better future life.

With man, and it seems to me with other animals also, a great intangible enters the process and insures that procreation will also be creative. This element is love. Love desires good for the offspring, and desire is the greatest stimulant to the seeking out and finding of the ingredients of success and attainment. Whether or not any trace of this magic element is found in the plant world would be a question difficult to answer. We cannot understand ourselves in such matters; how can we hope to understand an organism with which we have but a one-way communication?

Eternity, immortality, heaven and hell—these things are ponderables. They deal with future hopes and fears—fear that this earth may fail us in the end, hope that a new earth will emerge to save us. Physical scientists both frighten and encourage us. They see our sun as expendable—in time it will burn out, leaving us cold. But they also see millions of other suns and an expanding universe. That plants and animals see no "other worlds," acknowledge no end to this, does not mean they have no stake in the future. Plants and animals developed swift and sure means of travel long before man. While man dealt only in "angel wings" and "Jacob's ladders" the plants and animals managed to get around very well. They had already developed "intercontinental missiles," life-preserving "time capsules," ocean-spanning balloons and rafts. They had even discovered and made use of the jet streams. When man perfects his space ships and achieves interplanetary travel he may very well discover that plants and animals have beat him there. There is still a vast amount that we do not know. Search for the knowable unknown may well be one of the reasons for our existence. But the fact that plants, unknowing, still have a compelling urge to live as though they knew, may be sufficient reason why we should also.

4

AT THE SAME TIME THE PARADISE VALLEY firs were bearing their seed the mountain hemlocks were also developing a crop of beautiful purple cones about two inches long, which hung down in masses from all the branches of all the older trees, and higher up the white-barked pines were maturing fat, lopsided cones, green in color, which would supply the squirrels and birds with rich pine nuts throughout the long winter months. As pines require two years to develop their cones, on any one mature tree there are likely to be hanging, all at the same time, the small green cones of this year, the gray-green mature cones of last year, and the empty brown cones of several previous years.

The calliope hummingbird loves to build its dainty, dollar-size nest of cobwebs and thistledown on the side of an old white-barked pine cone, or on a knot on the trunk of the tree. This is effective camouflage, as the gray nest, often decorated with bits of cone scales and bark, is difficult to distinguish from the dead knots and cones of the rugged old tree.

Most conspicuous and showy of the mountain fruits are the orange-red berries of the mountain ash. People sometimes asked me during the summer: "What was that brilliant berry I saw so often on the way up here?" I checked with Ranger Flett, who knew more about the natural history of the park than anyone, and we counted at least a dozen plants with red berries that might have been seen along the road. These included the red evergreen huckleberry, the spiny devil's-club, the red elderberry, the bunchberry or Canadian dogwood, and a lot of others. But the berry most conspicuous in the upper valley was the mountain ash.

The mountain ash, which is the rowan tree of "Oh, Rowan Tree" and other English ballads, has been planted extensively in Seattle and other Northwest cities, where in spring its white flowers and in fall its masses of red "berries" lend beauty to the scene. It is a fair-sized tree. But the native mountain ash *(Sorbus cascadensis)* is a shrub and grows only in the high mountains.

The birds love the mountain ash berries and flock to the bushes, and since the "berries" are actually little pomes or apples they taste like bitter apples.

The fruit which pleased Ruth and the bears most, however, was the huckleberry or blueberry. They grew in masses on the subalpine hillsides, and when they began to ripen, a sort of huckleberry fever became epidemic in the high country. Not only did Yakima and Cowlitz Indians move up from the reservations and camp in the blueberry patches, but bear, with a long hungry winter in immediate prospect, used the occasion to fatten up their carcasses and fill out their hides as well. Birds flocked in from all directions; and even the ground squirrels began storing them away to add variety to their diet of seeds and nuts.

Ruth soon caught the fever. At first it was only a mild form of the malady. She gathered the plump fruit from the hillside behind our camp and we had blueberries and cream for dessert. Then the cook at the camp gave her a blueberry pie and her temperature mounted. I came home one evening from a trip to Pinnacle Peak and told her of the fields of berries around Reflection Lake and of the camp of Indians I had seen there gathering them by the basketful. Now the fever had her in its grip. The scattered bushes behind our camp led her down to the campgrounds; and the patches of berries there led her to the fields on Mazama Ridge. Soon she was spending days picking and canning blueberries. We could not buy jars at the camp store, but the hotel cook gave her mayonnaise and peanut butter jars and she filled all she could get. We had so many blueberries that six or seven years later we found a few remaining jars in our fruit closet and promptly threw them out. We were still fed up on blueberries.

There is always an argument as to which are "blueberries" and which are "huckleberries." Many people say that the high-bush varieties are huckleberries and the low-bush species are blueberries; and a commercial blueberry grower once explained to me the difference on the basis of the number of seeds in the fruit of the different species. Actually we have seven species of the genus Vaccinium or huckleberry, and six of them bear *blue* berries. The other, called red whortleberry by C. Frank Brockman (the botanist who followed me as Park Naturalist on the mountain and wrote the beautiful little government publication on the *Flora of Mount Rainier National Park*) is the only one that is *not* blue. By my definition all berries of the Vaccinium family are huckleberries, and the huckleberries that are blue can correctly be called "blueberries." The bears did not even make that distinction. All berries were fodder to them, and they stripped the bushes right and left, gobbling down berries and leaves alike.

One day while I was out on a guide trip Ruth was gathering blueberries near a little pond called Fairy Lake, a half-mile below our camp. There were loads of bushes there and she had two pails. When one was filled she set it on a stump where she could find it again and started filling the second pail. After a time she heard a commotion. The gray jays were squawking and something was floundering in the brush near the stump. She ran over and saw Blackie rolling in the bushes with the pail over his head. Berries were flying everywhere, and Blackie was clawing at the pail and trying to run backward at the same time. Apparently he had reached

Blackie and the blueberries

Blackie trapped

up to "pick" this particularly fine bunch of berries, stuck his nose in the pail, and then tumbled it over his head. The handle had fallen behind his ears like the elastic women used to use to hold on their hats, and he was stuck with it. He promptly forgot about blueberries and began concentrating on getting this diabolic thing off his head. It blinded him and he was scared. Ruth was angry about the loss of her berries, but she could not help but be amused at the fix Blackie's greed had gotten him into. There was nothing she dared do to help him because he had become a little buzz saw armed with sharp claws which were flailing the air. He would have torn her clothes off if nothing else. The struggle did not last long. He went tumbling down the hillside and soon came to a little ledge about ten feet high. He fell down this and landed so hard at the bottom that the pail flew off his head.

Blackie did not wait to gather any more berries but went yapping down the hill as hard as he could run. Ruth, glad he was not hurt, sat down laughing to watch the end of the adventure. On the flat near the pond he met his mother coming up. She had heard the rumpus on the hillside. The old lady wasted no sympathy on her cub but cuffed him savagely and drove him into the woods.

A little later they were playing together by the side of the pond. Apparently Avalanche Lily was trying to get him in the water for a bath. He seemed shy of the water, but after she had splashed around for a time he waded cautiously in until the water was up to his belly. The mother bear moved farther away and Blackie followed her. Suddenly she whirled around, grabbed the cub in her front paws, and soused him up and down in the pond. He struggled and bawled and tried to get away, but she held him, dunking and scrubbing him. Finally he got away from her, floundered out of the pond, and dashed for cover. At the edge of the brush he stopped, shook himself like a wet dog, looked once over his shoulder reproachfully at his mother, and ducked out of sight. She was sitting in the shallow water, smiling, apparently, to herself. The brown cub was nowhere to be seen. It was near dusk. Ruth came home with only one pail of berries.

Avalanche Lily and cub

5

ANOTHER PRODUCT OF THE ALPINE meadows which a few animals and many people enjoy is the annual crop of mushrooms.

Puffballs *(Colratia)* grow huge; *Agaricus,* the common meadow mushroom, is abundant in places, sometimes forming "fairy rings" in the meadows; and growing from the fir needles under the trees there is an occasional scaly red fly mushroom *(Amanita).* Down in the woods inky caps *(Coprinus)* and morels *(Morchella)* grow. There are the tasty oyster mushrooms *(Pleurotus)* growing on logs and stumps, a beautiful bear's-head coral mushroom *(Calraria),* and many others whose names I never learned. Of course there are also bracket fungus *(Polyporus)* or "conk" growing on dead trees, but these are woody forms that hold little interest for anyone except forest pathologists.

Many people in the Northwest, especially the Japanese Americans, relish the tasty fungi and eat them for breakfast, lunch, and dinner when in season. They make annual expeditions into the high country just to gather mushrooms.

One day in late summer I met a family of mushroom gatherers coming down the hill as I was going up to our camp. They had a large pail full of the fat red Amanitas! I stopped to chat and examined the mushrooms. According to my book the fly mushroom *(Amanita)* is deadly poisonous.

I asked: "What are you going to do with these?"

"Eat them," they said. The family were, from their looks and talk, not too far removed from Mediterranean origin, possibly Italian.

I shook my head. "Those are poisonous," I told them. "They will make you sick."

"Oh, no," they said, "veery good," and went on down the trail. It worried me, and I got a Seattle *Times* next day at the inn and looked for a headline saying, "Entire Family Wiped Out by Mushroom Poisoning," but I did not find it.

Since then I have read that certain Siberian natives use this species as a narcotic and go on terrible jags from eating it, and recently an article in *Harper's Magazine* entitled "Toads, Mushrooms and Schizophrenia" describes similar practices.

The things we call mushrooms, of course, are only the fruiting bodies of the fungus. The plant proper is a mass of threadlike "stems" called mycelium which grows in the partially decayed duff or dead wood of the meadow or the forest floor. Some fungi are parasitic and grow on living plants, and these cause diseases. The fungi reproduce and spread by means of spores produced by these fruiting bodies.

The fungi are classed as primitive plants. It is quite likely that they are plants which have degenerated from a higher order, since they have no chlorophyll and are therefore parasitic and saprophytic.

Fungi are the chief agents of decay in the forest, and for this reason they are of prime interest to the forester. As the man said about women, "We can't live with 'em and we can't live without 'em." Without the services of fungi in bringing about the decay of dead wood, and their cooperative function (still little understood) with the roots of trees, there could be no new growth; but they also, through disease and mechanical injury, kill many living trees.

Disease in the forest is not ordinarily serious. In fact, it is on the whole good for the forest, since it removes inferior and stunted growth that hinders the best growth of the sturdy trees. But when it gets out of hand and becomes epidemic it may wipe out entire species. It was a fungus-caused blight *(Endothia parasitica)* which killed all the chestnut trees throughout the Eastern states a number of years ago, destroying 300 million dollars' worth of good lumber as well as removing a beautiful and immensely valuable shade- and nut-bearing tree from our parks and forests.

One of the most dangerous forest diseases in the West is the white pine blister rust *(Cronartium)*—also the result of a fungus. The white pine is a magnificent tree in the Northwest, where it grows only as an occasional specimen scattered through the predominantly fir and hemlock forests of the mountain and all along the coast, although it is abundant in some parts of northern Idaho and western Montana. Sold as "Idaho white pine," it is that state's chief lumber-producing species.

White pine blister is caused by a fungus plant similar to that which causes wheat rusts.

The development of special reproductive cells called spores is only one step removed from the simple cell division of the lowest plants, but spores, as used by the fungi, have to contend with a great variety of conditions, such as drought and extremes of temperature. To survive these sometimes adverse conditions, they have devised various methods of self-preservation. In its simplest form this may be only a tough protective covering for the spore, and in its most complex it may, as in the wheat rust and the white pine blister rust, involve the production of several sorts of spores, a primitive form of sexual interchange, and an alternation of hosts. The wheat rust, for example, grows at one stage of its life on the common barberry, and the blister rust grows during an intermediate stage on the leaves of gooseberry and currant bushes or on other species of the genus *Ribies*.

This habit, which is life insurance from the standpoint of the fungi, provides the forester with his best method of controlling the disease. He has simply to remove all the gooseberry and currant bushes in the vicinity of the white pines.

The actual life history of the blister rust is fascinating. This so-called primitive plant grows as a long threadlike mycelium in the tissue of the tender white pine twigs, taking nourishment from the cells and so stunting growth or killing the twig.

6

IT WAS NEAR THE END OF JULY before I got a chance to make the summit climb. By now I felt quite confident of my ability to handle a party in almost any circumstances. I helped Hans and Heinie off with a large party one warm afternoon when as it happened I had no scheduled trip out, then I went back to the guidehouse to work on equipment. There were always shoe calks to be reset, clothing to be dried, gear to be stowed away; and there was always the possibility that someone would show up in need of a special guide. This day it happened. About the middle of the afternoon a big husky-looking individual came rushing in. He was in a terrible hurry; he wanted to make the summit climb and he could not wait. He had only two days to spend—he wanted to spend them dangerously.

The guide manager told him that both summit guides were on the mountain—the party having left soon after noon. This would-be climber suggested that he was in wonderful shape and a good walker and he could easily overtake them. The manager asked me if I would accompany him to Camp Muir to join the summit party there.

We outfitted hastily and one of the junior guides was sent rushing over to the kitchen for lunches. By four-thirty we were off. On the way up Alta Vista I stopped off a moment to tell Ruth good-by, then rejoined my "client" whom I shall call Bill as I do not remember his name.

Bill was still in a hurry and tried to set the pace. He wanted to reach Camp Muir before dark. He also talked all the time—mostly about himself. I have long held the opinion that the quickest way to expose ignorance is by way of the mouth so I talked very little and insisted on a slow steady pace such as Hans had taught us. Although I had never been over the trail before, I had often watched climbing parties through field glasses or the hotel telescope. I was sure that I knew every foot of the way, and the manager had been careful not to mention the fact that this would be my first ascent.

There is a pony trail to Panorama Point, which lies a little above timberline. At this point we left the trail and headed straight across the snowfields for Camp Muir, three thousand feet above, and three miles beyond. There is no great danger in this area—it is just a long hard grind. Within an hour Bill was breathing heavily and not talking nearly so much. He wanted to stop occasionally to rest, but I was out in front and I kept up the slow hard pace. I wanted to make Camp Muir by dark also.

It normally takes four or five hours to reach Camp Muir, which is at the ten-thousand-foot level. By nine we were a few hundred feet below the camp and I "halloed" to Hans. Hans answered with a yodel and came part way down the trail to meet us. Heinie had hot cups of strong, smoke-flavored tea ready for us. Most of the party had already turned in, so we got Bill bedded down as soon as possible. Heinie would be up at midnight melting snow and boiling tea again.

In August of 1888 John Muir and a small party, guided by P. B. Van Trump (who had accompanied General Hazard Stevens on the first successful ascent eighteen years earlier) camped at this point. The old master of glaciers and mountains had selected the site because the presence of a bed of light pumice indicated to him that it was sheltered from the more violent winds. This, I soon discovered, did not mean that the spot was warm. A. C. Warner, who was the photographer with the Muir party, tells of building stone windbreaks behind which the party found shelter for a few hours during the dark of the night. Several of these shelter walls still stood. In more recent years a small stone hut had been built by the guides. Boards and tar paper for the roof had been packed up from Paradise on men's backs. But our party of eleven people more than filled it. I took my blankets and bedded down with Hans and Heinie in one of Warner's "goat beds" outside.

I was too cold to sleep, so I lay huddled in my blankets looking up at the hard bright stars which filled the black glasslike sky. I had never seen so many stars at one time before, and I marveled at the mystery of outer space and the apparent unreality of the arctic world around me. Silence was the most conspicuous element of the scene. Silence is an awesome thing—few people have ever experienced it. Quiet is soothing, creative, therapeutic, but silence, the utter lack of sound, is frightening. I have experienced almost total silence only twice in my life, once for an hour alone in a diving bell 365 feet below the surface of the ocean, and again for a brief period when left alone two thousand feet underground in a coal mine. Both times there was sound, but only the sound of my own pulse in my ears and the faint whisper of my breathing.

Camp Muir that night was noisy by comparison. There was the wind, and occasionally the weird cracking and groaning of the glacier. But there were periods of almost total silence, and it was my first conscious experience of the absence of sound. It was as though in the unnatural vacuum of

Oscar at Camp Muir

sound the voice of reality thundered in my ears. I think I would not have slept even had I been more comfortable, and at midnight I welcomed the sound of Heinie building a fire and putting snow on to melt for tea. Later I got up, put on my parka and wool cap, pulled on dry socks and my heavy boots, folded the blankets, and went inside to wake the party.

Most of them were already awake and sat up when I lighted a candle. Someone asked what time it was. I told them, "Almost one." Several people groaned. A woman said: "There was an animal in here last night. It ran over me."

Hans, who was getting sugar out of a locker for the tea, said, "That was Oscar. He lives here."

"Who the heck is Oscar?" another asked.

"Oscar's a friend of mine. He's a mouse," Hans replied.

Actually there were several white-footed deer mice living in the chinks of the cabin, where they had warm nests lined with cotton stolen from the mattresses.

I asked Hans how they got up there. I can hardly imagine a tiny mouse making the four-mile trek over the snow and ice from the nearest meadows below, and although they lived well on scraps of food left by summit climbers during the brief climbing season, there were some nine months of arctic winter during which no food was imported from below. Hans had no idea how they got there. Mice do not hibernate and most mice do not store food, but the next spring Oscar, or some of his relatives, were still at Camp Muir. It is a mystery in survival that I have not solved.

There is an unconfirmed report of a black bear being seen crossing the summit in a snowstorm, but I think it was an hallucination. A big white billy goat looked in the window of the Anvil Rock fire lookout station a half-mile down the cleaver from Camp Muir one summer, and a dead robin was picked up on the snow at thirteen thousand feet by climbers in one of my parties. I have seen a sparrow hawk near Camp Muir, and that may account for Oscar. He could possibly have been carried by a hawk and in some way escaped him, but it is more likely that he hitchhiked a ride in some climber's pack. The guides always carried a small bundle of firewood on top of their pack to be used as fuel at Camp Muir, for there was no other way to secure water than to melt snow. The weight of an extra mouse or two in their pack would not be noticed by either Hans or Heinie, I am sure.

Hans liked to get away from Camp Muir by one or one-thirty. We had an hour of safe climbing to the Beehive and by then it was usually light enough to see. The trail follows up a rugged backbone of lava called Cowlitz Cleaver, which separates the Nisqually and the Cowlitz glaciers. Camp Muir is at its lower end and Camp Comfort, above Gibraltar Rock, is at its upper end. We used a rope out of Camp Muir to keep the party together in the darkness, but the first time we needed it as a lifeline was at the Beehive—a tall spire of rock which rises from the Cleaver. Here, using the rope, we climbed some thirty feet straight *down*.

For a distance then we climbed up the edge of the Cowlitz on ice so steep that Hans had to chop steps with his ax. This is slow going and cold, since moving the party one at a time makes for much waiting. By daylight we were climbing rock again in the vicinity of Camp Misery. Camp Misery is only a small, relatively flat place on the Cleaver at 11,033 feet, where a number of climbers have bivouacked, but never comfortably, I think. The name is entirely appropriate. If Hans or Heinie had tried to sleep there their feet would have stuck out over one of the glaciers.

At Misery we ate a second breakfast of hardtack, raisins, nuts, and chocolate from our summit lunches.

There have been so many summit parties since that one that I do not remember the people well. There were several women, one who was gray

The author climbing at sunrise on Cowlitz Cleaver above Camp Muir. (Photo by Rounds)

and one who was very young and pretty. I remember her. My man, Bill, had calmed down markedly and had melted into the group. He was carrying about fifty pounds of excess fat, and even though he was a big man he did not carry it well. But so far he had not complained. Neither was he bragging about his fitness. No one talked much even when we stopped to rest.

Here at Misery Hans treated us to some fine yodeling, because the echoes from eleven-thousand-foot Little Tahoma across the glacier are good. This and the food cheered us some, but the young girl (call her Nancy) was the only one, besides Hans and Heinie, who had any bounce left. Hans was always witty and cheerful, and Heinie made people laugh with his clumsy-ox ways and his heavy German accent. But either Hans or Heinie was a good man to be roped onto in a rough spot.

The most dangerous and most frightening part of the climb lay just ahead—the traverse of Gibraltar Rock. Hans warned us to keep close together and keep close to the rock. This second warning needed no verbal emphasis for most of us, for the ledge is narrow and at places the rock overhangs so closely above that it is impossible to walk upright. Hans and Heinie crouched, and some of the party crawled on all fours across the tight spots. Above, the cliff is so steep that you can see only a few feet up, and below there is empty space for a thousand feet down to the Nisqually ice. The most dangerous thing, however, is falling rocks and the ice and loose rock that lie on the ledge.

Beyond the Gibraltar ledge there is a three-hundred-foot scramble up the icefall called the Chutes. Here, however, a rope is anchored each spring and left until fall. With Hans and Heinie taking turns cutting steps, and the fixed rope as well as the climbing rope to hang on to, it is just like going upstairs. A constant shower of chipped ice from the lead guide's ax is bothersome but not dangerous. In another hour we stood at Camp Comfort, the last rock, which lies in the saddle between the top of Gibraltar and the broad dome of the summit.

From Camp Comfort, where you first feel the warmth of the sun, if there is a sun, the route lies over snow to the rim of the crater. This is hard but safe going except for three or four huge crevasses which cross the trail. Here we roped the party on two ropes, Hans taking the forward party and Heinie the second. I brought up the rear. Bill was just in front of me. Nancy and the gray-haired lady were on Hans' rope.

Because of the altitude and the exertion of the steep climb Hans set a very slow pace. Almost as in a slow-motion film he picked up his huge boots and set them down again, kicking each in a few inches above the other. All the rest of us stepped in his ample tracks.

The first crevasses we crossed on a snow bridge. Hans went first, moving very slowly and cautiously, ready on an instant to dive forward and flatten out if there were any sign of the bridge failing. Heinie and I tended his rope, belaying it around our ice axes. Safe on the upper lip, he set his ice ax handle deep into the frozen snow and anchored the line to it. I anchored the lower end. Then with one climber at a time on the second rope Heinie eased them across. The next summer Hans saved an entire party of climbers at this crevasse, and three years later a guide lost four men in it.

Now we were stopping often to rest. It was difficult to breathe. Bill wanted to sit down in the snow but Heinie would not let him, so he would lean on his alpenstock breathing heavily. After a minute or so the guides would pull up on the rope and call out, "Come on now, we're almost there." By the time we had made thirty or forty steps we had to stop again. Our gray-haired lady was sitting in the snow and Nancy was trying to help her. Whenever Hans would call out, "Let's go," Nancy would yell "Allez-oop" and start counting steps. It is a joy to have such a person on a

Climbing party led by chief guide Hans Fuhrer just leaving Camp Comfort, at 12,675 feet, for the summit. Paradise Valley and the Tatoosh Range are far below. Pinnacle Peak, 6,562 feet, is in right center. (Photo by Ranapar Studio)

summit climb. Her zest and enthusiasm were contagious and made the ordeal lighter for everyone in the party.

At the second and third big crevasses there were no safe snow bridges and we had to go several hundred yards to the right, and then to the left, to get around them. Hans and Heinie decided that they would some day build ladders to bridge them and thus save perhaps a quarter of a mile of hard traversal. Later in the summer I carried a two-by-four, eighteen feet long, from Camp Muir to Camp Comfort, which was my share of the terrific job of getting two ladders to the summit of Mount Rainier.

It was almost midday before we saw the barren ridge of lava which is the south rim of the summit crater. By now Hans was carrying the gray-haired lady pickaback, and it was no longer possible to keep Bill on his feet at the rest stops. For the last hundred yards or more he was unable to get up at all and crawled on all fours the ten steps Heinie called for between stops. At the crater rim, which we reached soon after twelve o'clock, Hans and Heinie tried to make the party comfortable in the shelter of the huge rocks flung out by the last violent eruptions. They fed and tended their charges as though they were small children. Very few, least of all Bill, were much interested in the scenery so far as I could see.

This is not the actual summit of the mountain but there is a bronze cylinder here chained to a rock containing a Mountaineer Club register. Hans brought it out for all to sign. After eating our lunch of boiled eggs, hardtack, chocolate, and nuts (the guide lunchboxes contained extra eggs and an orange), Nancy and I ran down into the crater and across to the other side. Here we climbed up another hundred feet to a dome of snow on the west rim of the crater which is Columbia Crest, the highest point. (At that time it was shown on the map as 14,408 feet, but a recent survey makes it two feet higher—whether from accumulated snow or more accurate measurement, I do not know.) This is not the highest point in the United States, as it was thought to be when named Columbia Crest by H. E. Holmes of the 1891 Ingraham party. It is, however, only eighty-five feet lower than Mount Whitney in California.

When we reached the summit and looked back we saw that Hans was waving to us to return, so I barely had time for a quick survey of the vast panorama stretching from Mount Jefferson in mid-Oregon on the south to the Pacific Ocean beyond the snow-capped Olympics on the west, and to Mount Garibaldi in British Columbia on the north. Puget Sound lay like a map spread below us, and the sister peaks—Adams, Hood, and St. Helens—along the Columbia River looked very close, although the nearest, St. Helens, is forty-seven miles away. Below us the fourteen great rivers of ice flowed down and out like the fingers of a white hand spread wide.

When we got back to the crater rim, Hans had already started down with the slower members of the party and Heinie was waiting for us with the others. Hans had to get us below Gibraltar by two o'clock if possible, and Bill and our gray-haired lady had slowed us dangerously.

The two-thousand-foot face of Gibraltar Rock has a southwesterly exposure. There is snow on top and on warm bright days the sun melts some of this snow. Water running down the cold face of the rock seeps into cracks and in places forms huge icicles. There were some as large as telegraph poles and half as long. Water freezes in the crevices and, expanding, loosens chunks of rock. At about two o'clock on July afternoons the sun hits the face of Gibraltar and melts this ice to water, again freeing the rocks. Sometimes also the huge icicles fall. Frost is erosion's sharpest tool and this is the way mountains are made into plains, but it is very dangerous to people who happen to become involved in erosion's machinery. There were so many accidents and so many close calls from falling rocks at this point that from 1939 until 1948 this route was abandoned by summit guides and the longer Kautz Glacier route used instead. However, no easier route has been found and most parties still climb over Gibraltar.

We got down safely and at Camp Muir, where I stayed behind for a few minutes to tidy up, I caught a glimpse of Oscar. He was sitting on top of the food locker nibbling at a raisin held in his white paws. I left a few extra tidbits for him and Mrs. Oscar and soon overtook the party on the Muir snowfield.

7

IT WAS ON MY NEXT SUMMIT CLIMB that we had the experience of almost losing an entire party. This was the largest party we ever attempted at one time. Again Hans led it; Heinie was second in command; and there were three assistant guides, Tommy, Wes, and myself. There were seventeen climbers, if I remember correctly. It was a slow party, naturally, but there had been no problems on the way up except the usual one of overcrowding at Camp Muir. One of the party said later, "We slept like spoons, nested. Whenever we turned over we had to count off, then all turn in order down the line. We even had to synchronize our breathing—half of us inhale as the other half exhaled." We were literally packed in like sardines, and it was so cold and windy out that Hans sat up in the doorway all night. I squeezed in with the others. I remember telling Ruth the next day: "I slept with a very nice lady last night—I've forgotten her name."

It was well after noon before we got started down from the summit, and Hans was very much worried about falling rocks at Gibraltar, so he was hurrying as fast as he dared. We had spliced three ropes and we were all on a single line, Hans at the head, Heinie and Tommy among the climbers, and Wes and I about twenty feet in the rear as anchor men. Hans was taking long sliding steps in the soft steep snow and some of the short-legged people were literally running. Every so often someone would slip and fall and be dragged to his feet again by the rope. We had crossed the upper crevasses safely and were at a very steep place about a hundred yards above the big crack. By now this one was twenty feet across at the top and had become a *bergchund*—the ice had slipped away leaving the upper lip about ten feet higher than the lower and almost overhanging it. Along the upper lip was a narrow level shelf, a cornice, which was all that could be seen from above.

On this steep slope someone slipped near the upper end of the line and slid in under the others, knocking several people off their feet. This knot of people struck the rest, knocking the guides off their feet also, and soon the entire party was sliding. Wes and I called out, and digging our ice axes into the snow threw our full weight upon the handles, riding them down. Then the rope broke and the party in one scrambled heap cascaded toward the big crevasse. Only Hans was still on his feet, legs braced, plowing snow and trying to hold the avalanche of human bodies. Wes and I were left far above—there was nothing we could do but watch, and I couldn't watch. I closed my eyes.

When I opened them again Hans was sitting on top of the pile and they had stopped in a heap not ten feet from the lip of the cornice. Without a word that I heard he got to his feet and started out along the upper ledge, heading for the snow bridge and pulling the people into line along the rope behind him.

It was at this crevasse and in about the same manner that a guide party fell three summers later, killing four men.

8

I AM NOT AT ALL SURE THAT PROXIMITY with death in any way prepares one for the event itself. The keen edge of reality is so difficult to accept that nothing but extremity will cause us to face it.

So although each one of us walked every day where the slightest misstep would hurl us to certain death, we were all profoundly shocked when one of the guides fell from Unicorn and was killed.

It was Paul's first year on the mountain; his first year in America also. He was not a professional guide like Hans and Heinie, but he had had a great deal of experience climbing in his native Switzerland.

He was six feet four or five, and he had a tremendous reach. It was because of this that we thought he might be able to make the ascent of

Unicorn Peak, highest of the Tatoosh Range, from which the guide Paul Moser fell to his death. Mount Adams, 12,307 feet, stands in the distance. (Photo by L. D. Lindsley)

the northwest face of the Unicorn, a route which had stopped even Hans and Heinie. Paul was eager to try it.

I remember him as a good-looking chap with dark hair and a ready smile. He was thoughtful and willing about the guide-house, and courteous to members of his parties in an Old World manner which charmed the ladies. But men liked him also; he was popular with us all.

The first fair day he had free he headed for Unicorn Peak, taking Joe, one of the junior guides, with him. Joe told me parts of the story and the rest I saw. It was a day we will never forget.

They left the guidehouse at eight o'clock, carrying only ice axes and a small rucksack with their lunch.

Climbing up the Pinnacle Glacier Paul suggested that just for practice they try the north face of Pinnacle Peak, which at that time no one had scaled, but Joe thought that Unicorn was all they had better tackle in one day, so they went on. From the Saddle, below Pinnacle, they followed the backbone of the Tatoosh to Unicorn Peak, 6,939 feet high and tallest of the range. Unicorn lies about three miles east of Pinnacle.

There is nothing difficult about Unicorn except the hundred-foot horn at the summit, and it is not too difficult from the backside. The north face, however, is so steep that it seems to, and perhaps actually does, over-hang the two-thousand-foot cliff. Snow Lake, fed by the small Unicorn Glacier, lies under this face.

Paul surveyed the sheer rock face, said that it would be easy, and im-mediately started up. It looked very difficult to Joe, and he hesitated. About thirty feet from the top Paul, who was out of Joe's sight at the moment, called down that he would have to take off his shoes, the hob-nails were too slippery on the hard rock. Joe climbed up to meet him and took the shoes, placing them on a small ledge.

Paul climbed back up the chimney, then started around the bulging face of the cliff. He soon came to a place where he could proceed no far-ther. He tried a half-dozen different positions and holds and finally called down, "I can't move here." Joe then climbed up the shallow chimney to a point just below him and Paul said, "Let me step on your shoulder." Joe was in a good position, solidly braced, and so he said, "All right . . . , go ahead."

As Paul reached down his left foot for Joe's left shoulder, he suddenly swung backward and out from the rock, falling past Joe. He struck first only about twelve feet down, but rolled off the ledge immediately and fell out of Joe's sight. This first cliff is about five hundred feet high with a thousand-foot rock slide at its base. Joe heard a small avalanche of rocks started by the falling body far below.

He had to go down several hundred feet before he could see the face of the cliff, and he was now several hundred yards from it. He could see no trace of the body and, certain that Paul was dead, he hurried down to Reflection Lake and the trail back to Paradise. He was running now, and near exhaustion. At the top of Mazama Ridge he fell and lay for a time to catch his breath. A boy came by, and Joe asked him to run to Paradise Valley and tell the guides that "Joe is on his way home—alone." The boy ran.

The accident was reported immediately to Park Headquarters at Longmire, and Rangers Macy and Greer, who were in the valley at the time, were assigned to head a rescue party. I was out on the Stevens Glacier; Hans and Heinie were on the mountain. The doctor put Joe to bed.

Rangers Macy and Greer climbed to the foot of the horn, where they found the ice axes left there by Joe and Paul, then they worked their way down and around the north face, trying to determine where the body would have fallen. Just before dusk they found him, terribly torn and broken, and spent the entire night getting the body down to Snow Lake.

At the guidehouse that evening we talked of sending a second party, but Joe was still sleeping, and we had little information. We doubted if we could even find Snow Lake in the dark. At dawn the rescue party got in. Ranger Macy was new on the park and this accident so depressed him that he determined to go back home to Kansas at the end of the season and lead a saner, safer life as a farmer. Fortunately he did not. He is now superintendent of the park.

9

ECOLOGY IS THE NAME GIVEN BY BIOLOGISTS to animal and plant sociology—it is the study of relationships between plants, animals, and their environment. In other words, a study of plant and animal communities. Just as people have preferences as to where they shall live—the Swedes and Norwegians followed the logging camps across the Northern states to the fishing grounds of Puget Sound and Alaska because they found work and climate similar to what they had known in Scandinavia; the Greeks and Italians followed the sponge fisheries to Florida and the grapes and the sun to California—just so do plants and animals follow the sun, or the rock, or the swamp, to a new environment similar to the one their ancestors have found by trial and error to be friendly to their needs.

I had done some reading in animal ecology and later it became my chief scientific interest. For years I taught ecology at the University of Washington.

That summer on Rainier an interesting opportunity for ecological observation presented itself to me. The Paradise Icefield is a mass of ice lying immobile in a shallow cirque. Since it does not move much it is fairly smooth and unbroken, and since the annual accumulation of snow does not quite equal the annual loss from melting, the ice is slowly receding. Unless climatic conditions change, the Paradise Icefield, along with other similar ice fields at the same elevation, will eventually disappear entirely.

This summer a small rock appeared almost in the middle of the ice field about a half-mile from the southern edge, which is just above timberline ridge. I examined this island the first day I discovered it. Then it was only a yard across and as barren of life, so far as I could see, as was the earth on the first day of creation. Actually this rock was newborn land, exposed to air and light for the first time perhaps in more than a hundred thousand years. A mile to the west and with almost the same exposure lay McClure Rock, which is just above Panorama Point on the Skyline Trail. McClure has been free of ice for a thousand years, perhaps.

There at 7,500 feet elevation there are no trees as such but there is a fairly complex and extensive community of plants and animals. I was sure this new island would develop a similar flora and fauna, but I was interested to see how it came about and in what order the settlers arrived.

There are adventurous spirits among plants and animals just as there are among people. Which would be the first to invade and claim the new land? Perhaps it would be a bird who, like me, would see it from a distance, and being curious would fly over for a better look. The bird would not stay, just as I did not stay, but the bird might leave a seed and the seed might grow. Remember how Charles Darwin in an experimental mood dropped grass seed in a pool and later caught a fish from the pool and fed it to a stork. Then he planted the droppings from the stork—and grass grew in the new ground.

The pallid horned lark

But this was barren lava, hard basalt. How could anything grow? Plants may come equipped for just such problems; their root cells may secrete acids or enzymes that can digest rock; or they may carry with them bacteria capable of doing the same thing. But no doubt minute particles of soil had already arrived, carried by the wind from off the ridges which surround the icefield. This is apparent on the snow, which becomes dirty during the summer from wind-blown dust. With successive layers of snow the ice becomes marked by ribbons of dust. In this soil, which may contain minute amounts of organic material as well as the basic minerals, the little plants and animals of the glacier ice sustain a precarious life. Traces of this dust would lodge on the rock island also, so in time there would be enough soil in the crevices to germinate and support a wind- or bird-carried seed.

No doubt the first plants to settle on this island were invisible bacteria, and the first plants I expected to see were the primitive mosses and lichens. Actually the first plant I did see was a tiny grasslike sedge. On the upper side the snow was still higher than the rock of the new island, and on hot days water from melting snow trickled across it. This provided a suitable habitat for the water-loving sedge, seeds of which may have been carried on the muddy feet of a passing bird. Rosy finches, pipits, pine siskins, and the pallid horned lark are often seen far out over the ice fields on nice summer days. The white-tailed ptarmigan which rarely flies does not usually go far beyond timberline.

Within a month of its "birth" the area had expanded until it was ten feet across and three hardy plants were now growing on it. The second to arrive was the alpine willowweed, a tiny Epilobium, similar and closely related to the common fireweed. This plant, with its pink flowers, has a cottony seed readily carried long distances by the wind.

The third plant was a low, dark green moss. Insects were present now, beetles and spiders, carried also by the wind no doubt, so a small community was already established.

Next summer the area was fifty feet across and a hundred feet long, and some twenty-five species of alpine plants and animals were resident.

So, in the course of two brief alpine summers, a new land, a terra incognita, a virgin continent never before seen by the eyes of man, is discovered, explored, and laid claim by a hardy colony of pioneers who will in time tame and possess it. They will clothe its barren rock with grass and flowers, even trees no doubt, in which pipits and siskins will rest, and beneath which the mother ptarmigan may some day brood and rear her young.

As on McClure Rock to the west, the Lyall lupine may grow with yellow stonecrop and the rare golden aster highlighting its deeper blue. Purple duck-billed lousewort will blossom in moist spots, and starlike Tolmie saxifrage will bloom in the pumice beds. Two dwarfed but brilliantly colored paintbrushes grow here also, and the crowberry and yellow heather can be found. Alpine buckwheat and the tiny sandwort thrive, and a minute willow tree so dwarfed that a ptarmigan can feed from its topmost twigs is sometimes found. Strangely, most of these same species may also be found on the rocky tundras beyond the Arctic Circle.

Mountain goat may feed here then, and newborn kids with woolly heads and too long legs may romp and play in these new pastures.

But how does it "happen"? This company of twenty-five—how did they get here? Of them all only the birds perhaps came by intent; came because they reasoned it was a good thing or an interesting thing to do. The others came by "accident"; blown by the winds, carried by passing birds, washed down by water from above. Were they derelicts stranded on a barren island?

And *was* it accident that the seed of the sedge had a hard tough shell so that it would survive desiccation and mechanical injury and the searing heat of the sun until it "happened" to find a drop of moisture and a pinch of soil in a crevice of this barren rock? Was it accident that the tiny seed of the willowweed came equipped with a silken sail so that the wind would lift it and carry it long distances over snow and ice? Was it accident that the baby spider spun a filmy web which the warm air rising from the valley lifted and parachuted onto the new continent? Was it accident, even, that the wind, an agency of erosion and therefore one of the tools of creation, swept cinder and ash from the Cleaver and deposited it in the pockets and cracks caused by frost in the glass-hard basalt, there to absorb a bit of moisture melted by the friendly sun from the surrounding ice and so to form a trace of soil in which a stray seed could germinate and grow? And was it accident that this seed so promptly heeded the Biblical admonition to "be fruitful and multiply and replenish the earth," and so within a brief season bring a hardy second generation to the new land?

I wonder. Is there any such thing as "chance," and do accidents ever "happen"?

There is a fascination about this high alpine country which many men have felt but few have been able to express, since mountain men are more given to contemplation than to speech making. John Muir in his great love of the mountain fastnesses, and John Burroughs in his deep appreciation of the hidden meanings in nature's ways have most vividly made their feelings known in literature and so been able to share them with other like-minded people. As a student, the two rugged but gentle Johns had long been my favorite authors and many a journey to the college library for assigned reading in forestry or biology never got beyond the shelf holding their books.

10

DURING THIS SPRING AND SUMMER I had spent many hours around timberline and the fascination grew. Ruth shared this feeling to a degree and on my free days, if the weather was pleasant, we sometimes walked across Edith Creek Basin to the glacier rim or even to Panorama Point and ate our sandwich lunch in some tiny sun-drenched meadow sheltered by the wind-blown alpine firs, white-barked pines, and mountain hemlocks of timberline.

Edith Creek Basin—in winter a perfect ski bowl—is in spring and summer a sea of flowers. In addition to the fields of lilies, anemone, lupine, paintbrush, asters, mountain dock, false hellebore, valerian, buttercups, and cinquefoil or potentilla, it is always possible to find rarer flowers like the tiny blue veronica, the mats of Alaska spiraea, and the white rhododenron and rosy spiraea which grew as low shrubs at the edge of the clumps of alpine fir trees. Along Edith Creek itself and again as we followed down the roaring Paradise River on our return trip we enjoyed the masses of scarlet Lewis monkey flower or mimulus and the two varieties of the equally showy yellow or alpine mimulus. Here too I was usually able to find a few clumps of the tall-stemmed grass of Parnassus with its fringed petals, faintly veined with green and the pearl-like buds as white as snow. In moister places there were also caltha or marsh marigold with golden centers and waxy heart-shaped basal leaves, and purple and gold shooting stars, which are wild cyclamen. In such places I looked also for the dark purple spikes of the elephant's-head and the bird's-beak pedicularis or lousewort. The first has remarkably lifelike little elephant heads with flappy ears and extended trunks and the bird's head of *Pedicularis ornithorhynca* is equally striking. *Ornithorhynca*, the species

A clump of the elephant's-head lousewort. (Photo by L. D. Lindsley)

name, literally translated would mean "bird beak," but the species name *(groenlandica)* of the elephant's-head lousewort seems to be a Danish Latinization of "Greenland," where it is possible that ancient elephants once roamed, as they did in Arctic Alaska, and where this strange little flower grows commonly. *Pedicularis* means "a plant with lice," or "a lousy plant," and I consider that a libelous misnomer. There are numerous other, less spectacular, louseworts to be found in the park also.

In midsummer all along the way are great mats of purple heather or red mountain heath and rarer clumps of the beautiful bride's heather, or as the botanists insist on calling it, Merten's Cassiope. I would approve of

Cassiope as a species name without protest since it comes from the Northern constellation of the same name, or rather the beautiful Greek matron for whom both stars and flowers were named. Higher up on the barren ridges there is sometimes found a yellow heath so different from the others that it rates a distinct genus name. It is called *Harrimanella stelleriana*, having been discovered by the Harriman Expedition in Alaska, and named for the sponsor of that expedition and Vitus Bering's German surgeon-naturalist Georg Steller.

Just before the trail reaches timberline ridge it passes through a rim of rock and here the brilliant scarlet cliff pentstemon cling along with the golden stonecrop, harebells, and rock brakes. There are nine or ten other species of pentstemon in the park and all of them are beautiful flowers.

Between the clumps of gnarled and twisted alpine trees at timberline are barren patches of wind-swept pumice where ptarmigan dust themselves on sunny days and horned larks stalk about, and at the edge of the pumice field are mats of tough low-growing plants which form arctic gardens very different from the alpine meadows just over the ridge. Indian basket grass, a lily, grows tufts of wiry grasslike blades and mounts tall stalks of creamy-white flowers later in the year. A dwarf huckleberry blooms and bears fruit here and the ptarmigan pluck both the bell-like flowers and the blue berries without stretching their necks to reach them. A relative, the prostrate bearberry, also grows here and produces bright red berries which no doubt help tide the small arctic animals—the marmots, chipmunks, voles, and meadow mice—over the long bleak winters.

Growing right up to the edge of the snow and ice are mats of spreading phlox with blue-pink blossoms and Lyall lupine with furry leaves and purple flowers close to the ground. There are occasional flashes of golden color where the fleabane or golden aster grows and acres of small tough sedges with black and gold blossoms mixed with the creamy-white stars of the Tolmie saxifrage, and numerous species of "pussytoes." These attractive little plants with their green woolly leaves have gray woolly flowers which greatly resemble the underside of a tiny kitten's paw, or the rare alpine eidelweiss to which they are related. There are a half-dozen varieties of these. They are first cousins to the pearly everlasting growing just over the hill. I was always able also to find the bronze-leafed, blue-flowered alpine Jacob's ladder, the moss *Silene* or moss campion, pink *Smelowskia*, the rose-colored mountain buckwheat and the willow grass with its dense racemes of yellow flowers. Tiny willow trees six inches high grow here also, as they do on the barren Arctic tundra of Alaska.

Although we chose quiet days and deliberately climbed far above the sounds of people and passing cars in the valley, we were never entirely alone or beyond the sound of pleasant things. Nearly always there was a breeze in the trees and an occasional distant rumble of ice shifting uneasily on the upper glaciers. Nearer at hand there were the calls of birds and the "eek" of conies on the talus slopes below the ridge. Occasionally too a marmot would become worried by our invasion of his sovereign domain and feel called upon to protest in shrill whistling. This would start the birds and the chipmunks chattering, but a marmot on a warm day has no great capacity for confusion and soon all would be quiet again except for the stirring in the branches of the trees and the contented chirping of siskins in the bushes or pipits teetering and flirting, wagtail fashion, at the edge of the cliff. If we were fortunate a mother ptarmigan might lead her covey of tiny chicks, quail-like, into the open to feed on blueberry bells or search for insects among the mats of gray pussy's-paws on which we rested. Pipits nest in such tiny meadows, holding with the ptarmigan, who nests among the heather and blueberry bushes at the foot of the timberline trees, the altitude record for bird's nests on the mountain. Now and again we would be mildly startled into alertness by the bulletlike passage of a hummingbird and might even get a good look at the tiny bundle of brilliance if it paused to probe the throat of a scarlet painted cup or a pentstemon for a possible sip of nectar with which to sustain such high-tension living.

Crossing the back face of Pinnacle Peak at about this same elevation one day in midsummer, I discovered what I have always remembered as the most perfect wilderness garden I have ever seen. We were working our way along a ledge higher than that we usually followed when I noticed at the level of my right shoulder a little shelf covered with bright-colored flowers. I went back to take a second look. Here on the sheer face of the cliff where almost nothing, plant or animal, could find a resting place, on a spot of basaltic rock less than a yard square, nature had contrived a more exquisite little garden than any gardener could have conceived.

How enough soil even to germinate seeds, let alone grow plants, had ever accumulated on this exposed wall of rock I do not know, but here hundreds of feet above the upper edge of the meadows a scant square yard of soil had been made, and this was entirely covered by a mat of mosslike mountain phlox, with hundreds of dime-size, sky-blue flowers spread over the dark green mat of leaves and stems. Out of this grew a clump of the dwarf scarlet-bracted alpine painted cup, or Indian paintbrush. This is the smallest and richest of the numerous species of *Castilleja* and it grows in the most barren places. In addition, there were several clumps of the silky-haired Lyall lupine, with short racemes of deep blue pealike flowers standing only two or three inches high.

But to set it all off, to give the crowning highlight, there was one plant with a dozen blossoms of the rare gold fleabane, more tastefully called golden aster, which grows only at high elevations in the Northwestern mountains. These delicate wild asters grow close to the ground and are a scant half-inch across. Around the edges were the fleshy, succulent leaves of the stonecrop, bearing low cymes of a duller yellow flower far outclassed by the brilliance of *aureus,* the golden aster. And all this concentrated beauty was heightened, like a diamond in a platinum setting, by the grandeur of the mountains on every side.

11

AT THE COLLEGE OF FORESTRY and in the lowland woods where we did our field studies I had been conditioned to think of forests in terms of commercial products, of desirable and undesirable species, and in board feet of salable lumber or ton of pulpwood per acre. But I was above all that up here on the mountain. The timberline trees about us, and the graceful clumps of tall firs and hemlocks in the mountain meadows we looked down upon, were in no sense commercial species. Even to a logger they would offer no temptation to harvest or bring no vision of fresh-sawn lumber stacked neatly in piles. This was however the growing edge, and these were outriders of the forest. Just as, fortunately, there are men who are pioneers by nature, who feel cramped for room if they have neighbors on more than one side of them and who are always to be found in the midst of the thankless struggle at the farthest frontier, so there are trees born to be pioneers by nature, who are always the forest outposts and who also gladly give their lives that others who will follow them may live more abundantly. Their recompense is the joy of battle. These alpine firs and hemlocks are the Boones and the Frémonts of the forest. They scout out the new land, push back the frontier, and the rest of the forest prospers on the land they win.

Timberline is found in many places but the same struggle goes on wherever you find it. I have seen it at fourteen thousand feet on the great African volcanoes which sit astride the Equator and at sea level in the north where it coincides almost exactly with the Arctic Circle. There are similar forest frontiers at the edge of the sea or at the edge of deserts and here the enemy may be a physical barrier but usually it is climatic, expressed in a shortage of moisture. At timberline on Mount Rainier and in similar situations throughout the high mountains of the world, and also in some arctic regions, there is ample precipitation, either rain or snow, but the moisture is locked up during most of the year as ice. So in most cases the real enemy of the trees is *cold*. It is chiefly because of the shifting frost line (around 12,000 feet at 0° of latitude—the Equator—and at sea level at 66.70° —the Arctic Circle) that timberline varies in altitude and in latitude.

Each fall millions of winged seeds are released by the stubborn timberline trees. These, borne by the winds which sweep up from below, are carried out across the shoulders of the mountain. Many of them fall on snow and ice to lie cold and dormant until carried down to the valleys and deposited deep under glacial till. Most of the others fall on stony ground, on the bleak wind-torn ridges of broken lava that sweep down like iron ribs between the ice fields. Some are picked up by the birds and small rodents, some buried deep beneath winter snows, but most of them perish on the barren rocks. A few may fall on moist pumice that has accumulated in sheltered pockets in the rock, may even germinate and grow, but there is no soil there. If they survive the sun of their first brief summer they quickly perish in the winter blast that follows. Only one in a million may survive.

Early in the summer on McClure Rock I had found growing one such tiny tree, an alpine fir. This is five hundred feet and a quarter of a mile above timberline on Panorama Point and this was a real forest outpost, a desperate attempt on the part of a persistent nature to take new land, to establish a new frontier.

In the lee of the rock in a tiny sheltered cove where a morsel of soil had been deposited by the winds and the few mosses and lichens that grew on the rocks above, one seed had fallen and held on with the grip of desperation to the spark of life within its battered shell. During its first summer it had grown less than an inch no doubt. In the fall the gods of the mountain had been kind to the tiny seedling and covered it early with a blanket of snow that shielded it from the driving blast. In the spring the sun's rays, reflected and magnified by the surrounding rocks of the southern exposure, had revived the minute tree to a short new season of life and growth. And so for many seasons the little fir had struggled unceasingly to retain the meager foothold it had been allowed to gain. Its probing roots had reached into every crack and cranny of the broken lava rock and the autumn snows and the sheltering Cleaver had been its allies. For perhaps half a century this tree had grown and it was then no more than three feet high. But now the slow-growing tip had reached beyond the shelter of the ridge, and the wind, furious it seemed at the advantage gained, had in one fierce ice-armed blast swept the upper branches bare.

It still clings there to McClure Rock, but its crown is broken and dead and it can never grow taller. The snows that once sheltered it in winter have become a burden to it and the soil, always scanty, is no longer sufficient to its needs. As time goes on it may grow a little but it will only become more twisted and gnarled. Even so this tree may survive in spite of the armies of nature which guard the frontier. It may even lay down a bit more soil from its own falling leaves, and sheltered beneath its matted branches other seeds may find lodgment, and other trees may grow until in time a meager garrison may be formed that by sheer force of numbers may be able to stand against the fierce-fighting soldiers of the elements. Then timberline will be advanced up the mountainside.

Today, as the hardy little tree approaches a hundred years of age, timberline is still down at Panorama Point a quarter of a mile below it. In between is snow and barren rock, but each year the snow recedes a little and the rock expands. The war drags on. As opposed to human wars, it is a struggle that results in progress rather than destruction. The land that is won at the forest frontier is not laid waste, rather it is clothed more luxuriantly. The captives that are taken are not made prisoners, rather they are set free.

Fortunately for the trees the opposition is not continuous, there are seasonal lulls in the storms of battle. For about nine months out of every year the soldiers of the enemy have the advantage. The trees must bow down under their thrusts. Gales tear away or strip their branches, snow and ice crush them under its merciless weight, and the frozen soil starves them miserably. Only the most rugged are able to endure the hardships of the campaign. But for three months the enemy rests. Cold is less intense during the summer nights; during the day the sun, like Polynesian warriors whose joy is in the fight and not in the winning, shifts sides and fights with the trees and the flowers. Water is unlocked from the frozen soil and the winds are not so fierce and violent. During the summer new outposts are taken, new lines established, and old lines more firmly entrenched.

In lower valleys still stand the legions of the reserves. Safe in the shelter of their kind they grow tall and great; they hold the land they could not take. They send rugged columns struggling up the narrow canyons and post outriders who stand guard on the wind-swept ridges, but the battle is won or lost at timberline.

All men are, I suppose, philosophers after a fashion. I remember when I was only a child of perhaps six or seven that I used to slip out of my bed on a clear night and climb to the top branches of a tall pine tree before the house and there I would sit for an hour wondering at the great mysterious universe around me. Then I did not try to put my feelings into words—they needed no words to clothe them—and here high above the world of people and things Ruth and I did not discuss our feelings, but we were both acutely aware of the healing calm of the wilderness around us, of the forests below and the skies above, and of the great silent mountain which stood over us.

At that time I was only a few months and a few miles removed, in time and space, from the suffering of battle areas in Europe, and I still felt the physical and spiritual effects of it. Ruth had suffered emotionally during the war also, since our Quaker-trained consciences told us that war is a crime for which we are all responsible and for which we must all bear a heavy burden of guilt. But from our Quaker teaching we both knew also the value of quiet—of space, and calm, and silent places.

Since the days of that first glorious summer we often visit timberline and we never fail to thrill at the creative struggle we see going on there and the stories we read in the faces of the timberline trees. It is strength and inspiration to us in our struggle for a better, more abundant life, it is our balm of Gilead. And that summer we spent in Paradise Valley ruined me also as a commercial forester, for although I went on and took a degree in forestry, I chose courses in conservation and avoided the "production" angles of the profession. Later I turned to ecology and biology, and my professional work and teaching have always been toward the development of aesthetic and recreational uses of forests and the preservation of wilderness areas to maintain these values.

12

BY SOME OBTUSE ALCHEMY of the human mind, men often seem more capable of seeing shadows than the light which creates them. Shadows creep slowly across a flat landscape but race swiftly up the slopes of a steep mountain. It is a matter of the "angle of attack."

So summer was a shadow sweeping with the speed of a frightened doe up the slopes of Mount Rainier, chasing spring before it. Spring became a fleeting season, measured not by the calendar or even the inclination of the earth which governs the calendar, but by the steep mountain slopes which magnified the sun's rays, and the angle of their attack. Although spring did not come to the high valleys until early July, and by mid-July it was past, until the first of September patches and fragments of spring could be found if you searched for them.

Some of these bits of residual spring were found behind dense clumps of trees and on the north slopes of precipitous mountains where deep shadows held snowbanks all summer and the snowbanks held back the spring flowers. Others could always be found by climbing up the mountainside to the line of melting snow where the same thing was happening.

On the third day of September that year, when I climbed Pinnacle Peak for the last time, I found spots on the northern slope where heavy snowbanks had lingered long and rhododendron bushes were just bursting out in new leaf, while nearby the same species had already ceased to bloom, and tardy avalanche lilies were blooming side by side with the late fall gentians.

Some of these early flowers which were forced to bloom late were actually caught, along with the gentians and purple asters, by the early snows, and were therefore cut off from maturing their seed. So for some the tag end of spring was caught up by early winter, and for these the cynics were right who said that actually we have no summer in Paradise Valley.

autumn

THE WONDERLAND TRAIL

1. Paradise Valley	6. Cowlitz Divide	11. Storbo Camp	16. Sunset Park
2. Reflection Lake	7. Indian Bar	12. Burrough's Mtn.	17. St. Andrews Cr.
3. Box Canyon	8. Frying Pan Gla.	13. Mystic Lake	18. Lake George
4. Nickel Creek	9. Summerland	14. Carbon R. Sta.	19. Indian Henry's
5. Ohanapecosh	10. White R. Camp	15. Mowich Lake	20. Longmire Sp.

1

LABOR DAY WEEKEND MARKS the end of the tourist season on Mount Rainier and therefore the beginning of fall. For some reason the Labor Day holiday and autumn weather seem to come together. Frequently the first hint that summer is over is a sudden unexpected snowstorm. And although we often have weeks of lovely "Indian summer" after these first storms, the traveling public is convinced that the season is over and that the fall weather is dangerous. They are afraid they might get snowed in. Of course they might. We often were.

Actually, autumn in the high country is wonderful. The purple asters and blue gentians shake off the first snows and go right on blooming. Great masses of orange-red berries hang heavy on the mountain ash, and the huckleberry bushes and vine maples turn the hillsides into a patchwork quilt of warm reds, sunshine yellows, bright greens, and rich browns. The nights are frosty and ice forms on the pools, but the days are brilliant and the warmth of the midday sun is enjoyed again as it is at no other time except on those first balmy days of spring.

Autumn seems to be the time for park rangers and wild animals to get out and do things they have not had time to do during the busy spring and summer. The rangers go on long trips patrolling the park boundaries; and the deer and goat gather together in sociable bands to feed and rest in the company of their kind.

It actually took Ruth and me three years to complete our first cycle of seasons in Paradise. That first autumn, with the money I had earned as a mountain guide, we went back to the university and my study of forestry. Our first son was born that fall also, and although I returned as a guide the following summer, Ruth and Kenneth remained at a small cabin we had built beside Lake Washington near Seattle and visited me at the park only occasionally.

But three years later I had finished my college work for the time being; Ken was now completely ambulatory; and I had been given the choice job of District Ranger for the Paradise District. With this job went a cozy log ranger station on the slopes of Alta Vista, a shiny Park Service badge, an office with a desk, a horse named Susie, and a Stetson hat. There was a clear, cold spring in the clump of firs at the back of the cabin; and the front porch looked out over the entire valley. Ken played in the tiny stream from the spring; and Ruth sat on the porch, after completing her simple housekeeping duties, awaiting my return from the office or the trail. There were flower fields all around us and friendly people often stopped by. Ken waved to the people and smiled, and when they said, "Hello, sonny," he turned shy and ran to his mother.

It was immediately after the Labor Day weekend this fall that we set out on our big adventure—the Wonderland Trail. As a National Park employee I felt that I should know more about the remote areas of this great natural playground, but I had been reluctant to leave Ruth and the baby long enough to make the trip around the mountain. Now we thought Ken was big enough to go along, so we would make it a family party.

2

I BOUGHT TWO HORSES FROM DICK WILLIAMS, the Park Company wrangler, one for Ruth to ride and one to carry our gear. Ken would ride on the pack horse. Dick was glad to get rid of Adam, and told me later that he never really thought the old nag would last out the trip. Barney he hated to part with, but he was getting old too, and Dick did not think he could be safely used another season on the Skyline Trail.

Barney was a character as well as a horse, and he quickly became a member of our family. He was a small bay gelding with a blazed face and white stockings. He bore the brands of several previous owners, including Indian brands from the Yakima Reservation beyond the Cascades. He was probably born on the reservation, but he had spent many years in the park before we knew him.

Like many great men, Barney started his career in a humble way. He came to the park first as a pack horse. Weighing less than a thousand pounds, he was too small for most men as a saddle horse. Ben Longmire preferred burros—"jackasses" he called them—in his pack string, but he knew Barney well. As a "packboss" in the employ of surveyors and rangers he had helped to construct most of the trails which completely surround the mountain and reach into all corners of the National Park. When the

Barney walking a footlog

new shelter cabin was built at Camp Muir, Barney was one of the few horses that survived the treacherous rock and ice and the grueling task of packing hundred-pound loads up the five-thousand-foot trail from Paradise Valley. I never saw a braver or more sure-footed horse. I rode him across ice where I would not dare lead most horses. He would even walk a footlog across a stream. I have never seen another horse do that. I felt safer with Ruth or Ken on his back than I would if they had been on foot. And he was one of those horses that, no matter how hard the winter had been and how scanty the range, always looked smooth and well fed.

He had two habits, however, which were not always enjoyed by his masters. One was a mania for walking on the very outside edge of the trail no matter how many hundreds of feet down a misstep might hurl him. This likely came from his pack horse days—a horse dreads catching his pack on rocks or trees beside the trail. And he took the same diabolic delight in walking to the very end of a switchback before turning. On high mountain trails this sometimes meant that fully a third of him protruded over the rim of an abysmal canyon as he pivoted on four feet in making the turn.

Ruth especially was opposed to these habits, and she spent a lot of time and energy in unsuccessful efforts to correct them. The second bad habit concerned me more than Ruth. When Barney was in hand he was as docile as a kitten; anyone could ride him; but once he was free with the open range before him he was a cayuse again, a wild horse. Unless I could drive him into a corner, I had to rope him. I have spent as much as half a day swearing and sweating and trying to catch that horse. If I rode too close he would kick me viciously.

But with Ruth and Ken he was always gentle. One day when leading the horses to water I put Ken on Barney bareback for the ride. At the trough he was jostled by the other horses and Ken fell off, landing on his back underneath them. Unhurt, he pulled himself up by Barney's hocks and walked out through his hind legs. Barney never moved.

He would come into the kitchen if invited, and had long since learned to open barn doors to get at the feed bins. I never tried it, but I am sure I could have ridden him into the hotel lobby, up the staircase, and around the balcony without any damage to anything or anybody.

Being docile and sure-footed, he had been an ideal lady's horse for the popular Skyline Trail trip, but he was old now and his feet were tender.

I made two wooden boxes for our food and camp equipment and slung one on either side of Adam's pack saddle. A bedroll and a sack of rolled oats went on top of these, and heavy blankets and a tarp were thrown over all. Ken fitted snugly into the "diamond" of the tie rope on top of the load. I rode Susie ahead, led Adam with Ken and the pack, and Ruth brought up the rear on Barney. Barney never did approve of this protocol. He wanted to lead the string.

3

WE LEFT THE CABIN ABOUT TEN on a crisp, clear fall morning, intending to camp that night at Nickel Creek in Stevens Canyon.

The Wonderland Trail is from a hundred to almost two hundred miles long, depending upon which of the various loops you take, for in many areas there is a high trail and a low trail. The high trail, although more rugged and more scenic, is the shorter since it lies within the lower trail. We kept usually to the high trail.

Ruth had been only as far as Reflection Lake before. Riding down the switchbacks between Reflection Lake and Lake Louise, I showed her where a few weeks earlier I had been stalked by a cougar. I had gone fishing in Reflection Lake one summer evening, and having caught only two or three small trout there, I had gone on to Lake Louise a mile farther down the

Cougar

canyon. My luck was no better in Lake Louise and it was getting dusk, so I headed for home.

No one had been over the trail in the half-hour since I had come down it, so I could see my footprints in the dust. I was startled when I saw that over every one of my tracks there was a five-inch cat track. A big mountain lion had followed me down. I decided that I wanted to get home before dark and almost ran up the steep trail, looking back frequently to see if my sneaky friend was anywhere in sight. No doubt he was watching me, but I did not see him. Thinking of it later I am sure it was the odor of fish that the big cat was following rather than me, but the story was not inclined to make Ruth feel too easy about camping out that night in Stevens Canyon.

It was only ten miles, all downhill, to Nickel Creek, and we made camp well before dark in an ancient burn beside the clear mountain stream. We did not carry a tent, so slept under the stars.

I put a bell and hobbles on Susie and turned the horses loose to browse all night in the open burn. I did not sleep well because I was not certain what they would do. We were still too near home: they might decide to go back. Anticipating this possibility, I had put bars across the bridge at the Box Canyon of the Muddy Fork a mile up the trail. Here the Muddy Fork of the Cowlitz River coming down from the Cowlitz and Ingraham glaciers has fallen into a great gash in the rock, and thunders through a box canyon which is one hundred feet deep and less than twenty feet wide at the top. There is no way of crossing the Muddy Fork except by the bridge which I had blocked.

Still, when I could no longer hear the tinkle of Susie's bell, I thought that I had better get up and see what had happened to the horses. Ruth was awake also, and I told her what I was going to do. "I'll be back in a few minutes," I said. A full moon was just coming up over Cowlitz Divide to the east and I was able to see without a lantern, but I found no trace of the horses in the burn. When I went up the trail a quarter-mile I saw where they had come onto it and saw their tracks heading up the trail. I found them at the bridge stopped by my barrier. Driving them back to camp, I heard coyotes howling on the ridge above the creek, but I did not realize how long I had been gone or that Ruth would be frightened.

She was crying when I came in, but it was not from fright. The coyotes, which she imagined as big timber wolves, had scared her, but it was anger at me for leaving her in such "danger" that brought on the flood of tears.

I tied the horses this time and we got a few hours of sound sleep before daylight and time to get up.

4

THAT DAY WE CLIMBED TO THE TOP of Cowlitz Divide at about five thousand feet and then down, through the finest stand of timber in the park, along Olallie Creek to the Ohanapecosh Hot Springs Ranger Station. Here Ranger and Mrs. Baldwin made us comfortable in regular beds for our second night on the Wonderland Trail. Before going to bed we had a bath in the soapy, foul-smelling mineral waters of the hot springs.

Next day, with a good breakfast under our belts and a bag of Mrs. Baldwin's oatmeal cookies in my saddlebags, we packed Adam and started up the long steep trail which would take us to six thousand feet before dropping down to the high meadow at Indian Bar just below the Ohanapecosh Glacier.

In the woods we saw sooty grouse and on Cowlitz Divide there were many deer tracks and trails, but Indian Bar was goat and ptarmigan country. It was a dull day, however, and the wind was cold off the glaciers, and we did not see any wildlife except a few dour ravens, several marmots, assorted conies, ground squirrels, and chipmunks.

There was no place to block the trail here; it was all barren scree and meadow, so I drove the horses across Boulder Creek above the camp, hobbled Susie again, and turned them loose. If they started home they would have to pass our camp on the down trail and we would hear the bell. A hobbled horse makes plenty of noise with a bell around his neck unless he moves very slowly. Also I did not think that they would cross Boulder Creek by themselves. It is white water right out from under the glacier, and it moves so fast that large boulders are constantly clanking and pounding down the bed of the stream. It is not a safe stream to ford, as a moving boulder could easily break a horse's leg if it happened to strike it. We slept cold, but undisturbed by yapping coyotes or wayward horses.

All around us was the roar of falling water. Although most of them were not visible from our camp, there are thirteen waterfalls in Ohanapecosh Park. St. John's, Marie, Mary Belle, Twin, Basaltic, Trixie, and Margarete Falls were all below. Wauhaukaupauken Falls were nearby, and six unnamed falls were on the branches of Boulder Creek above us. All the "girl" falls were named by Ben Longmire for the daughters of E. S. Hall, the first superintendent of the park.

The trip next day was up and out of Indian Bar, through Panhandle Gap, and down across the Fryingpan Glacier to Summerland. It was one of our shortest, but it is easily the most thrilling trail of the entire circuit.

This is the highest horse trail on the mountain. It leads up Boulder Creek past Wauhaukaupauken Falls and then climbs the left bank above the glacier to 6,500 feet. Here it follows around the upper rim of an old cirque with only a tiny unnamed lake where the ice once sat, and out of the cirque into Panhandle Gap between the ragged Cowlitz Chimneys on the right and towering Little Tahoma on the left. Little Tahoma hides the mountain from this point and standing sheer four thousand feet above us looks like the Matterhorn from Gomergratt above Zermatt.

As we made our way slowly, switchback upon switchback, we entertained ourselves by trying to teach Ken to say some of the interesting names of the region. *Ohanapecosh* he had learned, but *Wauhaukaupauken* gave him something of a workout. By the time we got back home, however, he could roll off these jawbreakers and sundry other place names such as *Puyallup, Klapatche, Williwakas, Olallie,* and *Wahpenayo* as fluently as either Ben or Len Longmire.

Panhandle Gap is a narrow saddle, almost a door in the rock, and it is the gateway between the south and the north sides of the park. It is just under seven thousand feet and well above timberline. Spread out before us was the entire northern Cascades with volcanic Glacier Peak and Mount Baker on the far horizon. The snow mountains we could see beyond Baker were high peaks of the Canadian Rockies. We spotted a small band of mountain goat watching us from the upper Sarvent Glacier just below the Cowlitz Chimneys. They stood immobile as long as we watched them. There are few travelers on this trail so we were a strange sight to them, but they did not appear startled.

Here where only small clumps of gray-green *Smelowskia* and mats of Tolmie saxifrage were scattered across the wind-swept pumice slopes we saw the pallid horned lark *(Otocoris alpestris)* stalking about. These small alpine songsters have the habit of singing on the wing as do their European cousins, the skylarks, but this was no day for singing.

Above us Little Tahoma still hid most of the mountain, and the icy vertebrae of the ponderous Emmons Glacier sweeping down from the summit until lost in the depths of White River Canyon below us dominated the western skyline.

Immediately below was a half-mile of steep ice where our trail crossed the eastern lobe of the Fryingpan Glacier. This looked dangerous, so Ruth and Ken got down and walked while I led the horses one at a time down the steep ice slope. Ruth has a picture which she took of me at this point and which she cherishes. It is taken from below. I am striding down the glacier with Barney in tow. Little Tahoma towers overhead. With the camera pointed sharply upward and with me too close to the camera I look like a giant leading a Shetland pony. She calls it "Hannibal Crossing the Alps."

We all got down safely, but at the foot of the ice we faced another problem. To get across to the lovely bench called Summerland we had to ford Fryingpan Creek. Like Boulder Creek this one also was moving heavy boulders, and Barney refused to enter it. I had already learned to respect Barney's horse sense and hesitated to force him. It would be too bad to lose a horse at this point.

We waited for several hours, hoping that the flow would slacken in the evening since the glacier was in shadow most of the afternoon, but there seemed to be little change with the passing hours. We were on the terminal moraine of the glacier with no feed for the horses and no smooth place for our camp, so we finally decided to attempt the crossing. I took Ken in the saddle with me and after some difficulty I was able to force Susie into the roaring water and drag Adam after us. We crossed safely after some uncertain floundering on the shifting bed of the belly-deep stream, but Barney was still fearful. He was smaller than the other horses, and wiser— he knew it was not safe.

Finally, when I moved the other horses up the trail as though we were leaving him behind, Barney decided to risk it. Ruth gave him his head and he proceeded with great caution, working upstream. He made it safely and we camped in a beautiful meadow at the top of the rise. From Summerland the entire north face of the mountain forms a white wall across the sky. No other alpine meadow is as close to the summit snows.

A large Mountaineer Club party had camped at Summerland the summer before and we found their stone fireplace and rude tables awaiting us. Late summer flowers were still blooming, and the gray jays seemed to remember that campers meant handouts. They flocked around our camp waiting impatiently for the supper call. When food was spread on the table they swarmed in and had to be "shooed" away like flies.

The horses seemed content to remain close to camp. After being unpacked and unsaddled, they each hunted up a smooth bare spot to roll in and then began to feed in the meadow. For the first time we did not hobble Susie; we were certain that they would not cross Fryingpan Creek again and the trail ahead was unknown to them. All night, whenever I happened to awaken, I heard the tinkle of Susie's bell near at hand.

5

WE STAYED LATE THE NEXT MORNING to enjoy the view. The trail down Fryingpan Creek past Goat Island Mountain was a good trail but through woods and not especially interesting. I noted that the forests of the shady north side differ somewhat from those of the warmer south slopes. Timberline is five hundred feet lower down; hemlock is more abundant; and there is an occasional Engelmann's spruce *(Picea engelmannii)*. Along the flat, boulder-strewn bottom of White River Valley there were also numbers of lodgepole pine *(Pinus contorta)*. Here on the West Coast the lodgepole grows very unlike the tall slender tree of the Rocky Mountains, where the species got its name. Western trees of the species do not grow in dense stands, so are bushy and spreading, more like the white-barked pines higher up, or the piñon pines of the Southwest. Recently dendrologists are calling the West Coast variety *Pinus murrayana,* giving it species rating, but I can see no differences in the two trees not accounted for by site and environment. I would call them geographic variations of the same species.

White River camp, far down the valley, we found dirty and noisy. It was abandoned, having been closed for the season, so we selected the cleanest cabin we could find and went to bed. There was little feed for the horses in the deep woods or on the gravel bars of the river, so we fed them oats from the small supply we carried and turned them into the corral. The cabin was almost over the river and churning water and pounding boulders made it difficult to sleep. Early next morning we were happy to be on our way to the high country again, but before leaving the camp I wound up the Park Service telephone and called Ranger Jimmy Brantner at the Carbon River Ranger Station. I told him to expect us in about three days' time.

This day was wet and the trail long and monotonous. It took us six hours of steady climbing to reach an abandoned mining camp called Storbo Camp in Glacier Basin at six thousand feet elevation.

The mine, never a profitable venture except for the promoters, had been abandoned for years. The old bunkhouse built of hand-split shakes was hardly more than a roof over leaning walls, but by now an icy rain was falling and we were happy to have any kind of a shelter for the night. There was a rusty kitchen range and some old mattresses hung by wires from the ceiling. We looked forward to a good night's sleep. As it turned out we got very little, for no sooner had we blown out the candle and crawled into our bed on the floor than we realized that the place was jumping with pack rats. I can get on fairly well with a few pack rats, for I have

Pack rats at Storbo Camp

nothing of the feeling toward them that I have toward their domestic cousins, but to Ruth a rat is a rat, and here there seemed to be hundreds of them.

First we heard them tapping on the attic floor with their hind feet as if to gather the clans, and then they took over the joint. They ran over our beds; they tried to carry off our shoes; they seemed to be moving everything in the place except the kitchen range, and we would have sworn they were trying to move that. After trying for hours to get to sleep I finally got up and cut our one candle in half, then lighted a candle at each end of our bed. During the brief hiatus that followed we went sound asleep.

Next morning there were no pack rats in sight, but even the candles were gone. Moving cautiously, I stood on a box and pushed my head up through a hole in the attic ceiling. Around a pile of debris on the attic floor sat a pair of big-eyed, long-whiskered, furry-tailed rats watching me. I examined their cache and found, besides pine cones, stones, and other trivia: rusty spoons, beer bottle caps, and fresh chips from my woodpile. And on top of the pile lay my dollar watch.

Next day I wanted to take the St. Elmo Pass route where the trail passes over the Wedge, between the Emmons and the Winthrop glaciers at an elevation of 7,500 feet, but the weather was still threatening and the pass was hidden by clouds. It looked pretty cold up there for Ken and there was a chance of real trouble if we got into a blizzard. Also we had been told that the trail down the Winthrop beyond the pass was hazardous, mostly sliding rock along the lateral moraine of the glacier, so we took the longer Burroughs Mountain trail instead.

We were glad we did, for at seven thousand feet on barren Burroughs Mountain the wind was heavy and raw in our faces and the only signs of life were a few horned larks who barely moved out of our way as we passed by. We were happy to get down into Canadian Zone timber again at the terminus of the Winthrop. Here on the broad outwash of the terminal moraine the trail disappeared entirely, and we had only our U.S.G.S. topographic map to guide us across to the West Fork of Winthrop Creek, where we found the trail again leading up to Mystic Lake under Old Desolate Mountain.

The map showed a shelter cabin here at about 5,500 feet elevation but we had some difficulty locating it. It was almost dark when we found a fallen-down cabin on the far side of the lake. Ruth and Ken were almost exhausted after our two bad nights and the long hard trip over Burroughs Mountain, so I told Ruth to make up the bed and turn in and I would cook supper and bring it to them as soon as I had cared for the horses.

I had another reason for this unusual solicitude—I had noticed a few snowflakes in the air and I did not want Ruth to become frightened. After supper I lay awake for quite a time wondering what we would do if we got snowed in at this elevation. I was glad to see that Ruth and Ken were sleeping soundly. I was glad also that I had telephoned Ranger Brantner from White River Camp.

The wind had dropped and there were no wood rats or other vermin to bother us here, so we slept soundly. At daybreak I woke up and looked out. There was more than a foot of snow on the ground and it was still falling heavily. When Ruth woke I told her again to stay in bed and I would cook breakfast, but she saw the snow through holes in the gable and got up. She thought we should get out of there as fast as possible.

I was uncertain. I had never been over the trail across Moraine Park and down to the Carbon Glacier. Now with a foot or more of snow there would be no trail to follow, and the map showed some very rough going past the Northern Craigs and along the moraine of the Carbon. The snow was still falling so heavily that we could see only a few yards in any direction. But the map also showed another shelter cabin in lower Moraine Park which was only three miles away and five hundred feet lower down. Perhaps it would not be snowing there. We had the telephone line to follow, but I knew from experience that, since it often took short cuts across canyons or up cliffs, it could easily get us into serious trouble.

I decided to take Ruth's advice to get out of there right away.

The horses were quite willing, and we saddled and packed hastily. Ken was bundled in a blanket and looked like a little Indian papoose perched between the bedrolls on Adam's pack. Soon we were all white with snow as we rode silently across the meadows. I changed horses with Ruth this morning and decided to let Barney find the way down, checking occasionally with my map. Within an hour I felt confident that he would get us out safely for small signs here and there—a blaze on a tree, the wire, and the lay of the land—had convinced me that he was following the trail. He may have been over it before sometime and remembered, but I think it was his unerring judgment and an instinct for safe going that got us out. We did not see the lower Moraine Park cabin, but since the snow was not so deep here we kept on going.

At the rock slides below the Northern Craigs we heard a "Halloo" and soon saw Jimmy Brantner and his big bay horse, Bud, coming up the trail. As usual Ranger Brantner was walking. In his hand he carried a double-bitted ax.

Bud was a beautiful animal and the two all but lived together, but Jimmy seldom rode, and never packed him. If he had a pack he carried it on his own back and walked. Bud followed, carrying only the saddle and saddlebags. The horse never knew a bit and bridle—when Jimmy rode he rode with a hackamore.

The ax, so sharp that it was said Jimmy shaved with it, was his badge of office. He was never seen on the trail without it.

Ranger Brantner had lived for years at the isolated Carbon River Station. He had few visitors even in summer, and he seldom got outside the park. It was a lonely life, and that perhaps accounts in part for his affection for his horse. Certainly Bud was by all odds the finest and most pampered horse in the park.

Jimmy made us feel very welcome at Carbon River and turned the place over to us. The next morning he walked up the trail with us to the junction at Ipsut Creek, and from there we went on to Mowich Lake, which we reached about noon.

6

THERE WERE BOTH A RANGER STATION and a shelter cabin at Mowich Lake, and Jimmy had told us where to find a key to the station. Quite a few people hiked in to fish at Mowich, so Jimmy spent some time there during the season and kept the place stocked with food. He had told us to help ourselves.

We spent two beautiful days at Mowich. Deer came into the meadow in the evening, and trout were leaping for flies that danced over the mirror-like surface of the water. We did no fishing.

On the second day we left Adam in the corral, took Ken on Susie with me and rode up to Spray Park. Once above the timber, the day was remarkably warm and the sky was of the deepest blue. Nearly all the snow of the recent fall had melted, but in a patch beside a tiny lake we saw the fresh track of a bobcat. Spray Park is one of the most beautiful parks with a truly magnificent view of the northwest face of the mountain.

Kenneth Schmoe playing in a tiny lakelet in Sunset Park on the Wonderland Trail.
(Photo by Floyd Schmoe)

There are a number of little lakes which reflect the rounded dome of Columbia Crest.

We lay in the grass to absorb the warm sun, while Ken waded and splashed in a baby-size lakelet. Seventy miles away and across the pool of blue haze which hid the Puget Sound basin, the Olympics formed a jagged, saw-toothed horizon. Here on the northern slopes we found blueberries ripening still, and we picked enough of the sweet fat berries for our supper.

Coming down we stopped to see Spray Falls, the highest and most impressive waterfall on the north side. The trail drops down alongside the falls in a series of short, steep switchbacks and it is kept muddy here by the drifting spray. It then rounds Hessong Rock and winds along the very edge of Eagle Cliff and back through woods to Mowich Lake.

It was a long ride next day down through the forests to the Mowich River and a longer one up again to the shelter cabin at Golden Lakes in Sunset Park, but we arrived in time to get unpacked and make camp before suppertime. Then we walked among the fifteen or twenty beautiful little lakes while we watched a brilliant sunset forming in the western sky. Nearer at hand the bands of rose and gold moved slowly up the great snow dome of the mountain until finally only the summit snows glowed beneath a halo of light. Soon the cold blue curtain of twilight was drawn across the scene, and we walked back to the camp in the gathering dusk. To the west daylight still lingered, and the peaks of the Olympic Range cut like broken glass into the evening sky.

7

IT WAS BETWEEN SUNSET PARK and St. Andrews Creek cabin that we began having trouble with bees. There is nothing a mountain horse hates more, or which is more inclined to drive him stark raving mad, than a swarm of yellow jackets—called simply "bees" by mountain men.

Of the hundreds of varieties of wild bees there are some apparently that are born with an ingrown antipathy for horses, and as is usually the case in matters of hatreds, the feeling is mutual.

The only time Barney ever forgot his sense of obligation to his rider was when attacked by bees. Riding ahead on Susie I usually stirred up the nest, and Adam next in line got stung, but Barney, bringing up the rear, was the one they really swarmed over.

I don't know how many varieties of wild bees are resident in the National Park, but the ones that I most often came in contact with were small slim hornets with brilliant black and yellow-striped backs. They have a prodigious temper and their ability to retaliate either real or imagined hurts equals their temper. These are not paper-making wasps with hanging nests that can be seen and avoided but rather, like bumblebees, they build wax combs in the fir needles and other duff of the forest floor. When a man or a horse stumbles into their nest, the entire colony comes out shooting.

Ken and Adam attacked by bees

The trail from Sunset Park drops down more than two thousand feet to the deep canyon of the North Puyallup River and then winds around the tip of Klapatche Ridge to the South Puyallup. An old homestead cabin on St. Andrews Creek near its junction with the South Puyallup was our destination. It is in this lowland with its devil's-club swamps and its huge cedar trees that the horse-hating bees live their belligerent lives.

Barney with some sort of equine radar detected the first nest and stopped, throwing his head violently from side to side. When Ruth forced him he bolted ahead, but several hot-shot dive bombers zeroed in on him and made direct hits. Ruth could not control him, and he dashed past us, knocking Adam clear out of the trail and raking Susie and me violently in passing. The only thing Ruth could do was hang on, which she did with both hands. Finally he stopped running and put on a weird sort of dance trying to reach inaccessible parts of his anatomy with his mouth and stamping all four feet violently at the same time. For the next several miles he kept throwing his head about and cursing bees under his breath.

Just before we got to the cabin I raised a really hot swarm which exploded over Adam and Barney like a Chinese New Year. Adam jerked the lead rope from my hand and went bucking through the brush like a yearling. I was amazed at what the old nag could do at his age, and near the end of a long, hard day's work at that! The sling ropes came loose and baggage and camp gear were broadcast far and wide, but Ken pulled leather like a veteran cowpoke and he was still aboard, although badly shaken, when Adam finally stopped from sheer exhaustion.

Barney and Ruth had disappeared in the woods in the opposite direction and I could not ride herd on them both at the same time, so Susie and I took out after Ken. Susie got a few bites which she resented violently, but she did not bolt and we soon overtook Adam and rescued Ken. Fortunately for us the bees seemed to hate horses worse than people and none of us was stung. We gathered up the gear, remade the pack, and went on to the cabin with Kenneth, who had had enough of horses and bees for one day, riding with his mother on Barney.

I wonder why it is that the wild bees are so hostile. It may be that they have been robbed so often that all their native tolerance has been worn away. Few insects have so much to lose as the honey-making bees, and few insects wage such a constant struggle against vandals. Some birds, many other insects, several animals such as the bear and the skunk, and man, all like honey and have at one time or another been guilty of larcenous assaults on the little honey-makers. So far as I know, however, horses are not bee robbers; they are only bee haters. But the much abused bees, no doubt, like other rich individuals, soon come to be suspicious of all people and consider every stranger a probable highwayman. Their policy seems to be: "Shoot first and you won't have to ask questions later."

The forests and meadows swarm with insects of hundreds of different varieties, and few animals (for strictly speaking any animate thing is an animal) are so marvelously formed or do such amazing things. The only insects that I feel well informed on, however, are the insects with which foresters and lumbermen are concerned. These are the tree-killing or wood-destroying insects such as the tree-girdling bark beetles and the leaf-eating moths. There are a few wood-boring bees.

8

THE NEXT WAS TO BE OUR LONGEST and in some ways our most interesting day. The horses were standing up remarkably well, and so were Ken and Ruth. We were up before daylight and had a good breakfast of bacon and hotcakes. While Ruth tidied up the cabin I packed Adam, and by the time the first slanting rays of the morning sun reached the forest floor we were on our way.

We were rather expecting that Ken might object to riding Adam again after the go with the bees the evening before, but he made no protest. He had come to feel, apparently, that he and Adam belonged together and this was his own private conveyance. During the long hours on the trail Ken talked quietly to Adam and to himself. We never really knew what went on between them, but it was apparent that Ken became very much attached to Adam and that the feeling between them was mutual. Only a very hot bee would cause Adam to forget momentarily that he was responsible for the small boy on his back. When we called back to Ken, as we frequently did, and asked, "How you comin'?" he would only grin.

The trail follows down St. Andrews Creek past several unnamed waterfalls and then turns up the South Fork of the Puyallup River for three miles through dark forests. Much of the trail is swampy, and such stretches were hard going for the horses. In the worst spots the trail has been corduroyed, and this was even worse than the mud, for their feet sometimes slipped between the logs and there was danger of breaking a leg.

Finally we crossed the Puyallup at a deep ford and climbed quickly back into the more open country at Round Pass. Here there is a junction, with the right-hand trail leading steeply up to Lake George and

Barney at the summit of Pyramid Peak. (Photo by L. D. Lindsley)

the left-hand trail dropping down to Tahoma Creek. There was time to spare, so we turned up the Lake George trail for an hour's visit with Ranger Claude Tice, who was stationed there during the hunting season on game patrol.

Lake George, second only to Mowich as the largest lake in the park, is less than a mile from the park boundary. There are many deer in the area, and a small band of mountain goat have long lived on the summit and the faces of Mount Wow, which rises precipitously beyond the lake. Ranger Tice was able to point out a band of five who were apparently watching us, although they were almost a thousand feet above us on the face of the cliff. Goat have been shot a number of times by poachers in the park.

After a pot of coffee and a chat with Ranger Tice it was still only midafternoon, so we dropped back down the mile of trail to Round Pass and headed for Indian Henry's Hunting Ground, which was to be our last night's stop on the trip.

The trail, sometimes in the forest and sometimes across the boulder beds of the stream, climbs almost to the snout of Tahoma Glacier before crossing the creek and striking up through clefts in the sheer cliffs to the alpine meadows above. Along Tahoma Creek we saw our first beaver dams and ponds. In one place the animals had flooded the trail by their ambitious dam building, and we had to wade water for a hundred feet or so. No beaver were in sight; the noise made by trail horses is enough to warn most animals to take cover if they are shy, and beaver are not only shy but somewhat nocturnal in habits. The best time to observe them at work is late in the dusk of evening. We did see freshly cut trees and their big web-footed tracks at the edge of the pond. I was surprised to find that here they had cut a small hemlock and peeled the bark from parts of it. The preferred diet seems to be black cottonwood, willow, and crab apple bark, since there is no aspen in the park. This is mild fare compared to hemlock, which contains so much tannic acid that hemlock bark is one of the important commercial sources of this chemical. Their stomachs must be well tanned.

It was late afternoon and cool when we reached the ranger station at Indian Henry's, and the horses were happy to get out from under their saddles and roll in the short grass. We fed them the last of the bag of rolled oats, which Adam had been carrying so long, and had no fear that they would leave us during the night.

It was good to get into a regular bed again with a mattress under us, and to cook on a proper kitchen stove. There were a few white-footed mice in the cabin but no mountain rats. After the pack rats of Storbo's Camp, mice were small inconvenience. I remembered, and told Ruth, Victor Hugo's observation on the Creation—I think it is in *Les Misérables:* "The Lord made a rat. 'Oh, ho,' he said, 'I've made a mistake.' So he made a cat to correct it." We did not need a cat.

We stayed over a day at Indian Henry's. There were goat in the valley; we saw their fresh sign everywhere; but we did not see any that morning. The horses no doubt had frightened them.

After lunch we saddled Barney and Susie and rode up to Pyramid Peak at the head of the valley. On the way we stopped at Mirror Lakes to enjoy the reflection. There were ptarmigan on Pyramid Peak, and flocks of rosy finches were flitting from rock to rock.

From Pyramid Peak we had a wonderful view of Mount St. Helens and Mount Adams to the south. From this point Success Cleaver leads directly to Point Success, one of the three summit peaks. This route has been climbed a number of times, but it is hazardous enough to tax the ability of the most experienced climbers.

The six-mile ride down through the meadows and woods past Squaw Lake and Crystal Mountain, and over Rampart Ridge to Longmire next day went quickly, for the horses seemed to sense that they were heading home and we did not discourage them. Near Longmire the trail passes through heavy strands of trees where sword ferns grow as tall as the horses' backs, and many other varieties are found.

From Longmire I took the horses to pasture on Bear Prairie and we rode a government truck back to the cabin in Paradise.

9

ON THE STEEP PACIFIC SLOPES EXPOSED to the warm west winds, the annual precipitation, mostly in the form of wet winter snows and torrential spring rains, totals upwards of one hundred inches. This heavy rainfall is reflected in the dense vegetation of the valleys and lower slopes, such as those around Longmire Springs. Beneath the huge firs and hemlocks with their hanging mosses and gray goatsbeard lichen (*Usnea sp.*) there is a ground cover of shade-tolerant plants that is tropical in appearance and all but impenetrable to any animal larger than a mountain beaver or a marsh rabbit. Glossy skunk cabbage leaves are almost as large as banana leaves, devil's-club leaves are eighteen inches across, and all down logs or rocks are covered with a mat of mosses often six inches thick. This, with the festoons of moss and lichen hanging from the vine maples in swampy areas, gives the lowland forest something of a typical "rain forest" appearance. Certainly the most attractive plants of this dripping northern jungle are the ferns. In many places they almost blocked our trail with their slender, drooping fronds.

Everywhere two species are most conspicuous: the heavy, simple fronds of the sword or Christmas fern, and the more complicated feathery fronds of the lady fern. The soft, lacy leaves of the lady fern spring from the wetter sites and are sometimes six feet tall and ten inches across. Sword ferns, which grow from drier shady sites, are sparser and seldom stand more than four feet in height. I remembered my first view of the West Coast forests when a few years before I had come out from my boyhood home on the dry plains of Kansas, and topping the summit of the Cascades at dawn one morning saw from the car window green ferns standing shoulder-high on all the hillsides. It had rained during the night, but the sun was shining then and the light glinted from the wet glossy leaves. I felt that I had arrived in a new world all fresh and clean and just released from the Maker's hand. In Kansas I had known ferns only as pampered house plants or as background material for a bridal bouquet or a funeral spray. Here they covered the ground as far as I could see, and smaller species even hung from masses of growing moss on the branches or in the crotches of alders and maples.

Actually there are some twenty species of ferns found scattered about on Mount Rainier, where they grow from the lowest valleys to sites well above timberline. Those growing from the trees were licorice ferns, which also grow on mossy boulders and the faces of drier cliffs. Their heavy rhizomes, or root stalks, have a sweet licorice taste, which gives them the common name. Everywhere we went in the more open woods of the lower valleys we saw and admired the dainty rosettes of dark green, almost prostrate leaves of the deer fern. From these rosettes in early summer more graceful, stiffly erect, spore-bearing fronds appear. The only function of these leaves is reproduction. After the minute brown spores are matured and spread, these fronds wither away, but the basal vegetative fronds remain green and growing throughout the year even under the heavy winter snows of the mountain valleys.

All ferns reproduce by this comparatively simple process of bearing spores. I say "comparatively simple" because the most primitive asexual reproductive systems known, those that involve cell division only, are so amazingly complex that although botanists have studied the problem for decades and written volumes on their findings, there is still a vast amount to be learned.

On the underside or at the edges of reproductive fern leaves there form tiny brown pockets called sporangia. These are packed full of minute spores all but microscopic in size. Each of these granules, which can be carried for miles as part of what may appear as a cloud of dust, contains an embryonic plant. Under favorable circumstances of moisture and warmth, often in the dark shade beneath a decaying log or on the earth of an undercut bank, these spores may germinate and grow into a new plant. But it will not be a fern as we know it. There is always an intermediate stage—a small, green, heart-shaped, liverwort-like plant called a prothallium, or "preleaf." If this tiny inconspicuous plant thrives, it will in time produce two types of reproductive cells within its leaflike structure. One is a female cell containing an egg, and the other is a male cell which will produce many mobile sperm cells. When these cells mature the sperm will be released to swim like a minute tadpole to the egg. This can only happen if rain or dew has deposited a film of water over the prothallium. Fertilization takes place on contact and a fertilized cell, called a zygote, results. This new pregnant cell will then in due season produce an embryonic fern which grows from the dead body of the mother plant, looking for all the world like its grandfather but not at all like its parent.

This process, simplified and generalized here in a way to make a plant physiologist weep, is called "primitive."

In the dark misty canyons and on the spray-drenched cliffs beside waterfalls we saw and admired hanging gardens of delicate maidenhair ferns, and on dry rock slides around Lake George and similar sites where the sun strikes warm there were many lovely clumps of the common rock brake. These bushy ferns, which are bracken-like but far more delicate than the rank-growing brake of the dry burned-over lands, also produce spore-bearing fronds and greener, brighter, vegetative leaves. This is division of labor—a class of food-producing fronds that spend months and years at hard labor to support a few frivolous fly-by-night sisters whose only function is to produce a few million spores and release them to the wind. An interesting parallel exists here between plants and insects. The caterpillar stage of the moths, for example, serves the same function as the vegetative fronds of the ferns, while the egg-laying adult moths are comparable to the showy reproductive fern fronds. With plants, however, there is no intermediate pupal stage.

At high elevations, in fact extending clear up to timberline in places, there is an alpine species of the lady fern, much smaller and stiffer than its rank-growing lowland cousin; and the rock brake, just referred to, also grows up along the dry moraines of the glaciers to timberline and above. I had often seen them among the shifting boulders of the Nisqually moraines. The real mountaineer among ferns, however, is the lacy lip fern which thrives only at high elevations and therefore is seldom seen except by rock climbers who are likely too much occupied in finding their way up or down to notice a fellow Alpinist who apparently feels perfectly secure on the sheer face of the precipice.

Often too along the trail we noticed the triangular fronds of the mountain wood fern, which is common in the more open stands on the ridges, and the delicately beautiful oak fern of denser woods. The oak fern has a slender brownish leaf stalk that a few inches above the ground divides umbrella-like into three broad leaflets or pinnae of almost equal size.

A number of rarer ferns, such as the male fern, the brittle bladder fern, the holly ferns, and the tiny green spleenworts, also grow high on alpine cliffs that are sometimes overhung by glaciers.

10

ABOUT A MONTH AFTER WE GOT HOME from the Wonderland Trail trip (it was late October or early November), the government supplied me with a beautiful new Speed Graphic camera which I had asked for. I wanted to try it out on mountain goat right away, and the best place for mountain goat was Indian Henry's Hunting Ground on the southwest shoulder of the mountain where we had seen goat sign a month earlier. They were seldom bothered by people out there, so they should not be too shy. During the summer they stayed well above timberline, coming down only at night to bed in the uppermost clumps of prostrate firs, such as we had seen on Pyramid Peak, but now there had been heavy snows at timberline and the bands had moved to the alpine meadows a thousand feet lower down.

We decided to take horses and spend a week with the goats. My horses were then still at Bear Prairie, but there were several government horses available, and I told Herm Barnett that we wanted to use three of them the next Friday.

Thursday evening we made up our packs and I loaded my film holders. Friday morning was clear and cold. There was frost on the twigs and grass. I went to the stables to get the horses, and Herm told me that he had sent them all out to winter pasture the day before. He had forgotten that I wanted to use them. I went back to the cabin and we talked it over. I was still anxious to make the trip, so we decided to back-pack in. I thought we could reduce our gear to bare necessities, drive down the road to the Kautz Creek trail which was shorter than the Longmire trail, and still get in before dark. We would have to go slowly so that Ken could walk most of the way because Ruth and I would both need to carry packs.

By the time we rearranged our supplies and outfit, and made them up again into shoulder packs it was almost noon, but we set out anyway. We left our car at the Kautz Creek campground and started up the trail. I had never been over this trail before, but it was shown on the topographic map I carried, and we anticipated no trouble following it, even though, as it turned out, it was not a trail really but a track made by deer and by occasional Indian berrypickers.

For the first mile it followed the glacial stream through deep woods. There were beaver ponds and marshy areas with devil's-club and vine maple, but the track was not difficult to follow. I carried most of the stuff and Ruth helped Ken. He was a great walker for his size, but we were going no faster than Ben's string of burros, which was a steady two miles per hour.

Just beyond Tum Tum Peak the trail climbs out of the canyon and follows the rim through an old burn. Here the alpine alders, white rhododendron, and mountain ash grew higher than my head, and the trail became a bushy tunnel in places. This was hard going, and we were glad to get out of it into Hudsonian Zone meadows on the slopes of Mount Ararat. Ben Longmire found a stump on top of this six-thousand-foot peak that looked as though it had a cable burn around it. Ben said Noah must have moored the ark to that stump, so he named the peak Ararat.

But it was getting late in the afternoon. Ken was becoming quite tired, and Ruth could not carry him far at a time. In grassy areas the track disappeared entirely and we would not be able to follow it in the dark. It was getting colder, too, but we still had several miles to go and there would be no moon. We decided that we had best find a sheltered place, build a big fire and camp for the night, even though we had not brought blankets or sleeping bags, since there were plenty of blankets at Indian Henry's Ranger Station.

We found a safe place among rocks and started to make camp. While Ruth and Ken rested I gathered a huge pile of dry wood from dead and down trees. Then I opened my pack and looked for matches. I could not find them. I searched everything, went through all my pockets. There was not a single match. In hastily repacking our outfit we had somehow managed to leave them behind. This was serious. For once I saw the disadvantage of being a nonsmoker. It was already freezing. Without a fire, even with our heavy clothing, we would spend a very miserable night. No doubt we could survive it, and we might keep Ken warm between us, but it was dangerous. I decided to go on. I hung my pack on a dead snag where the bears might not find it, took Ken on my back, and we started up.

Soon it was so dark we could not see the trail. Fortunately we were now in open country and for an hour after dark I could still see the peaks against the sky, so we kept on up the mountain, moving slowly and resting frequently.

At last we came to a high cliff at about the 5,500-foot level. We worked our way cautiously along its base, almost feeling each step, and came to a cleft in the rock with a trail leading up almost like a stairway. It was steep but safe, and after a half-hour of climbing we came to the top and were in open, almost level meadows.

I knew this was Indian Henry's, but how to find a deserted log cabin somewhere in a thousand acres of parkland with numerous small lakes and scattered clumps of alpine trees? It was now as dark as the proverbial stack of black cats, and I could not even see the summit snows. Shallow water was already coated with ice and the air was sharp. We *had* to find shelter.

For an hour, with Ken asleep in my arms, we searched, literally with our hands outstretched, for that elusive cabin. Finally we stumbled upon the stable. I think I smelled the odor of horses and dry manure first, and then we found it. I knew the ranger station was nearby, and my feet followed the track directly to it.

It was a log cabin, one room and a lean-to kitchen. Both doors were locked. Herm had assured me that we would find the kitchen door unfastened. This did not stop us long. I kicked a board out of the door, reached in, and slipped the bolt that held it. It was good to be inside. We felt warmer already, but we were completely exhausted. It must have been around midnight by then.

Feeling our way we found the door to the main room and located the wood-burning stove. There was wood in the box behind the stove and somewhere there would be matches. But first I reached up and found the mattresses and blankets hanging by wires from the rafters to keep them out of the reach of mice and pack rats, and soon Ruth and Ken were warm and sound asleep on the floor.

Then I started an inch-by-inch search for matches. It was so dark I could not see my hand in front of my face, and I had no idea where they would have been left by the rangers who had used this cabin on game patrol since we had been there in September.

First I located the kitchen stove and felt in all the shelves and cupboards over and around it. There were emergency supplies in the kitchen, and I opened every coffee tin or box I could find. I spent an hour in the kitchen and then started an examination of the larger room. Finally I found a baking powder can full of matches sitting on a beam over the heating stove. Soon I had a kerosene lamp burning and a roaring fire.

I went to a little lake above the cabin, broke the ice, and got a pail of water. The friendly yellow light in the cabin window guided me back. I found coffee, sugar, and tinned milk, and when the water was boiling I woke Ruth and we sat by the stove and drank sweet coffee rich with condensed milk. Then we went to bed.

At daylight, which came too soon, I dressed without waking Ken and Ruth and hurried back down the trail for our pack. I wanted to get there before some hungry bear found it. At the top of the cliff below Mount Ararat I saw that we had found and climbed the only possible route up. If we had missed the golden stairs we would have been down there in the canyon yet.

The pack was easily found and was intact. In an hour I was back at the cabin, but Ruth was up and had a fire going in the kitchen stove with water hot in the teakettle. Ken was sleeping curled up like a hibernating chipmunk, and still in his little parka and wool socks.

11

THE DAY WAS GLORIOUS. Everywhere the huckleberry bushes were scarlet, and the first snows had melted, leaving a few late flowers still blooming. It was a belated Indian summer day. I started out looking for goats, and Ruth began unpacking our stuff and cleaning up the camp.

There were goat all over the place. I counted twenty-four in small bands here and there within an hour or two. They were on Mount Ararat and on Pyramid Peak and also on Crystal and Iron Mountains to the east of the meadow.

I saw a big billy near the point where the Wonderland Trail breaks through the cliffs above the Tahoma Glacier, so I began stalking him. He watched me approach until I was about a hundred yards distant; then he quietly moved over the brink of the cliff and disappeared. I started down

Above:"The old billy disappeared over the rim of the canyon. It was only a hundred yards but it was a hundred yards straight down, and I did not follow him." (Photo by Floyd Schmoe)

Opposite: The large billy goat on a cliff below Indian Henry's Hunting Ground where he took refuge to escape the author's camera. The white mountain goat is one of the strangest animals on Mount Rainier. He is an expert climber and usually very shy. (Photo by Floyd Schmoe)

the trail, watching on either side, but I could not see him. After a quarter-mile, which took me several hundred feet below the crest, I started back up again. Then I saw him perched on a ledge of what seemed to be a sheer face and not more than a hundred feet above me. But it was a hundred

feet straight up, and he knew I was not coming up after him, so he simply stood and looked at me. I examined the cliff carefully and I could see no possible way for a monkey, let alone a clumsy-looking four-footed ruminant, to arrive at that perch. I never got closer to him, although I got a good picture of him on the cliff.

Every once in a while I receive through the mail from Japan a letter or a parcel with an eight-yen stamp on it. This brown Japanese stamp bears the picture of a strange animal that I have seen only in the Tokyo and the Seoul Zoological Gardens. It is a rare "mountain antelope" *(Capricornis)* with a shaggy mane. In Japan it is called *kamoshika;* in English a serow *(Naemorhedus crispus)*. There are a few left wild in the "Japan Alps" and in the mountains of Korea.

This is the Oriental representative of an interesting group of rare animals scattered widely about the world but never found in large numbers anywhere. The best-known representative of this strange band of sure-footed mountaineers is the chamois *(Rupicapra)* of the European Alps. Another is the heavy-horned, light-footed ibex *(Capra ibex)* of Europe and the Middle East.

In America we have the white mountain goat. The word "goat" is a misnomer. The genus name *Oreamnos montanus** is from the Greek God of the high mountains, Oreas. Shaggy and bearded, he looks like a cross between a goat, a musk ox, and a college professor—but he is not a goat.

So far as I know these are the only members of this unusual family, and of them all the white mountain goat is perhaps the most numerous. At present small bands of these rugged dwellers of crags and ice fields are found in high mountain pastures from Cook's Inlet in Alaska to the Columbia River, and east in the Rockies to Glacier National Park in Montana. Not in historic times has their range been much more extensive.

On Mount Rainier there are perhaps five hundred of these animals, and we found them the most fascinating characters of all our wilderness neighbors.

During our first days at Indian Henry's the goat were not overly shy and they were not posting lookouts. I tried to be quiet and unobtrusive, but I was persistent. I followed them around all day and got several long shots of them with my camera, but no close-ups. I decided that I would have to be either smarter or luckier.

*Now called *Oreamnos americanus americanus.*

Wolf chasing a goat

After a few days of this they began showing signs of nervousness. I thought it was my dogged tracking that was upsetting them until I discovered the track of a big wolf on Ararat. He had been chasing goat. The tracks were as big as those of a German shepherd dog, and although I did not find that he had made a kill, he must have frightened them more than I did. After this the bands began to consolidate and to post lookouts. This is a safety measure that has been learned by many hunted animals. Usually with the goats it was a wise old nanny that stood lookout, but not always.

On about the third morning—I had found that the goats were feeding at daybreak and hiding during the rest of the day—I left the cabin at dawn. There were no goats to be seen in the meadow, so I expected to find them along the rim of the canyon overlooking the glacier. I headed for a grassy ridge between two rocky points. I figured they might be just over this ridge. As I approached the crest I dropped to my belly and crawled along the frosty ground. At the summit I lay behind a big rock and very cautiously peered over. There, not a hundred yards below me, a band of about fifteen goats were feeding. Rather, they *had been* feeding. Now they were bunched together, and every goat was looking directly at me. There were several kids between their mothers' legs, and they were looking also. I lay there for several minutes trying to figure this out. I knew they couldn't see me. I had been so careful in my approach that I was sure I had made no sound. There was not a whisper of a breeze to carry a telltale scent. Yet they *knew* that I was approaching and they were looking directly at the point where I would appear. Somebody told them!

Then I looked at the point of rock on my left. There stood an old billy half-hidden in a clump of timberline trees. He was the lookout, and no doubt he had been watching me since the moment I left the cabin. I doubt that he called down: "Heads up, folks, that suspicious character is coming again." But animals do have means of communication. Perhaps they only watched him and by his attention to me they knew when and where I would appear at the crest. This is part of the herd instinct.

When I tried to move closer they all disappeared over the rim of the canyon. I went and looked down but I did not try to follow them. Goat can go places men were never intended to go. Far below I could hear an occasional tinkle of falling rocks and some gray jays scolding. When I looked for the billy he had disappeared also.

It may have been that same day, or a day later, that I accidentally cornered two young billies on an overhanging ledge of rock. This was on the opposite side of the valley, and they were looking down on the trail we had come up in the dark. They had a magnificent view. The Kautz Creek Canyon dropped away for three thousand feet below them, and beyond the Tatoosh Range and High Rock, Mount Adams loomed big against the sky.

I don't know how it happened that I surprised them. They seemed to be enjoying the view, but I doubt if it was mountains they were looking at. More likely some nice little nannies were across there on Rampart Ridge. Anyway I walked up to within a dozen yards of them before they saw me, and then they were trapped. They dashed about wildly for a moment, looking for a way down, but to go over that ledge was suicide even for a goat. They would have fallen a hundred feet free and then rolled for a thousand down the talus slope. In such situations deer and horses can be stampeded to their death, but the mountain goat are more like a donkey—they don't lose their heads easily. They would not long survive in this country if they did.

I stood still, for I had command of the situation, and after a moment they calmed down and stood facing me not ten paces away. It is the closest I have ever been to wild goat, and the setting was ideal. Two of them, framed in the rugged timberline trees, and the huge dome of Adams off there in the sky to give perspective and grandeur to the scene! I raised my Graflex, focused carefully, and pressed the release. At the whirr of the focal-plane shutter the goats abandoned caution and dashed past me not more than an arm's length away. They quickly disappeared among the rocky ledges.

I examined my camera. . . . "Holy mackerel!" I was the dumbest fool—I had not removed the slide from my film pack holder. I will never forgive myself. No wildlife photographer, before or since, has ever turned out such a picture of mountain goat as I muffed that day in Indian Henry's.

12

THE TRACK OF A WOLF WHICH had been chasing goat on Mount Ararat caused me to look into the matter of timber wolves in the park. Obviously they are of rare occurrence, and there is a question as to whether or not any still survive in the area. If it is true that the big wolf is extinct on Mount Rainier, then the track I had seen was that of a coyote or a large dog that might have wandered into the park from some ranch down the Nisqually. A domestic dog track of the same size could not be distinguished from a wolf track, and a coyote running through loose pumice and ash might make a track that looked as big as a wolf's. The fact that there was no kill strengthened this possibility, for although Ranger Flett thought that hungry coyotes sometimes kill young deer and goat, rabbits, marmots, ground squirrels, and grouse are game nearer their size. I have even seen a coyote reduced to the point of stalking grasshoppers, and a fat vole or mouse is never below his dignity.

Flett saw two wolves on Mazama Ridge in 1916, and the National Museum in Washington has the skin of one killed at Bear Prairie in 1897, but that was a long time ago. Gus Anderson said he saw a big gray wolf walk across the meadow at Longmire Springs early one morning during the past winter, and government hunter Charlie Stoner of Ashford, who has hunted "varmint" in the area for twenty years, said that he thought there were at least twenty-five wolves still hunting in the park, although he had never killed one there. Everyone agrees that coyotes are increasing in the area, that red foxes are holding their own, but wolves are no doubt on their way out.

This has been the history of the native wild dogs in every area—with the encroachment of men with their hunting dogs, their traps, and their poisoned bait, the smart little cousins of the wolf survive amazingly and even increase in numbers, but the big wolf fights a losing battle. There are areas in Europe and Asia, however, where the wolf has held his own against all enemies for hundreds of years, and every winter, even in densely populated countries such as Italy, wolves come down out of the mountains to prey on the farmers' sheep and goats.

At the time of which I write both the Biological Survey and the Fish and Game Department of the state paid bounties on the larger predators, including the eagle; and the Federal government maintained professional hunters to keep them under control. Because of their supposed damage to the deer and mountain goat, the National Park Service allowed cougar and bobcats to be killed within the National Parks, and in some parks, where they were more numerous than on Mount Rainier, coyotes and wolves were also hunted.*

We got up early next day for the long hike back to Longmire. It was much easier going home for we were not rushed for time. It was mostly downhill too, and we carried very light packs, having left all food (except our noonday lunch) and all other spare equipment at the cabin in Indian Henry's. Ken walked a great deal of the way and chatted, often to himself or with the birds and small animals of the trailside, in a very grown-up manner. We were amazed at the amount of knowledge and understanding our little human cub had acquired. Already—he was just past three years of age—he knew all the animals and many of the trees and flowers by their correct names.

13

KNOWLEDGE IS A HUMILIATING THING. Ignorance is also a humiliating thing—the word is the same but my meaning is different. Knowledge should make one humble; avoidable ignorance should make one ashamed—these words are very different.

*This is no longer the practice in any National Park.

In packing up to leave Paradise Valley I discovered in the folds of an old jacket hanging on the back porch the woolly web spun by the expectant larvae of a moth to protect its pupa. (*Pupa* means "doll.") I tore the glossy capsule out of its insulating muff and put it in my shirt pocket. It was immobile and appeared dead and cold, but I knew that it was only sleeping. At lunchtime I remembered it, and using a razor blade I sliced it in two. All I could see within the chitinous shell was a pasty yellow substance with no apparent form or pattern. With a hand lens I could detect a granular texture to the mass, but still no form.

Here was *stuff.* To an ignorant person just "yellow stuff," perhaps even "nasty stuff." Stepped on, it would be a "dirty spot on the rug."

But I knew that I was looking at the very stuff of life itself, and was seeing it in the moment of creation.

I had dissected insects before in the laboratory. I know that the larvae of a metabolic insect, a caterpillar in this case, is a highly organized, highly efficient, and tremendously energetic feeding machine with a one-track mind completely absorbed with the idea of eating all it can in order to become an adult as quickly as it can; and that the adult moth is equally complex, equally obsessed, and fully as efficient in its mission of the reproduction and the dispersal of its species.

The fact that the caterpillar is woolly and the moth gaudy is not incidental—nothing is incidental. Every detail is purposeful. In this case the spiny "wool" of the larvae protects it from insectivorous birds, and the brilliant colors of the adult lure the opposite sex with honorable intentions. Part of this obsession with growing up is this device of the pupal stage, whereby the insect quickly and safely by-passes the entire danger-packed adolescent period of other animals—a biological feature that the distraught parents of many a teenager would consider a wonderful idea.

But during this metamorphosis, this short cut to maturity, amazing things take place—things that dwarf in their significance such human achievements as atomic reactors and space ships.

Without even push-button control, without will or reason, the high-voltage life of the caterpillar pauses suddenly and lurches into the job of becoming a grown-up insect. After brief but frantic preparation to insure protection during the helpless pupal stage, the caterpillar changes before your eyes (if you are fortunate enough to be in on the secret) from an active, bright-colored "worm" to a dull brown capsule that appears as dead as a mummy in a case, and looks a lot like one.

But this little brown "doll" is far from a dead and embalmed mummy. Inside the rigid case, miracles are taking place. The entire internal structure of the animal breaks down and dissolves into this semiliquid stuff. A complicated nervous system, digestive system, and circulatory system disappear into an amorphous mass and appear again in due course, completely reorganized into a very different biological machine, intent now on an entirely different program of activity. The digestive system has all but disappeared, and instead most of the abdominal space is given over to an amazingly potent reproductive system. With almost explosive energy the new animal bursts from its protective mummy case and flies away a moth, with wide functional wings, long legs, sensitive antennae, compound eyes, and all the equipment necessary for smelling out a mate (experiments have shown that a male moth can detect the presence of a desirable female by smell alone at a distance of two miles or more) and producing a new generation of young.

It is one of the most amazing feats of an amazing nature. It would be no less surprising to one who had no advance knowledge of what was to happen if a green frog should suddenly climb out of his pond, roll himself into a ball, and shortly thereafter blossom out again and fly away as a robin or a chickadee. The nearest thing I know to this metamorphosis is the change in a toad or other amphibious animal from the free-swimming larva or tadpole form to the adult land-dwelling animal—but that is a poor comparison.

Change, of course, is of the nature of things. Nothing stands still. Creation spirals upward, death skids abruptly downward. To stand still is to invite disaster. Scientists who are philosophers (and what true scientist is not?) believe that all things have changed. Light is a possible exception, since the light generated millions of years ago by distant stars and reaching earth only now seems to have the same characteristics as the light which is generated currently by our nearby star, the sun. But nowhere else in my experience is change more spectacular, more mystifying, more visibly creative, than in this everyday occurrence—this metamorphosis of the common insects.

Daily we had been aware of change on all sides of us. During the long winter it had been slowed and muted, but it was still there. Quietly within the dormant buds, within the resting seeds, and within pregnant animals, embryonic life had been stretching and stirring. With the first breath of spring it would burst forth into new leaves, new plants, new life.

On the face of the mountain we could see change also. As the seasons came and went, the tools of erosion carved deeper and deeper—the flooding runoff of each spring's thaw, like the rings of wood laid down each season by the great trees, were the ticks of the clock of time which marked its life span. Summer then, following closely on the heels of spring, brought a season of fulfillment, of blossoming forth, and that was followed again, reluctantly, by the tucking in and drawing together of autumn. But this was not for the end, this was for the new beginning. After the winter of rest and of firming down, the cycle of the seasons would spring up once more and another year would be ticked off by the clock of time.

So time had passed—but time was also eternity and eternity was time—time that had been, time that was, and time that was to be! Paradise, like eternity, was here and now. We, in that vast realm of the mountain, had found our special paradise. For us it was a good life in a good world—a marvelous world of living nature, an expanding world of miraculous growth. And this should be the joy and the privilege of all men—a paradise to be sought, and if sought, to be found. Few perhaps like us can, or will, seek a paradise in such a wilderness, although a wilderness has much to recommend it. And ours of course was not the only wilderness—nor the only paradise. For the farmer there is the warm productive earth beneath his plow; for the educator and the philosopher the rich depths of the human mind; for the research scientist the limitless fields of his microscopes, his telescopes, and his Geiger counters; for the politically minded the vast forum of human affairs; and for even the simplest of men, unless they deliberately choose the life of a hermit, the warmth and comfort of a community of friendly neighbors—for if a man is friendly he will have friendly neighbors.

But even for those who found their paradise in other places our paradise of the mountains and meadows had much to contribute to theirs, and every season they came—by the millions—to spend a day or a week with us in this solitude.

Just what we found that made of this wilderness a paradise for us is a thing difficult to put in words. There had been adventure with thrills aplenty, but the greatest adventure we had found was in living.

Through four seasons we had dwelt beneath the spell of bold beauty. We had gazed across majestic landscapes bounded only by the fading blue of vast distances. Our horizon had been as wide, it seemed, as the world is wide. And all about us had been the towering heights which awed and inspired us. Even the dome of the sky had seemed bigger and brighter. Here also we had found elfin beauty—jewel-like flowers hiding the deepest mysteries of life behind their bright faces, winged seeds pregnant with immortality, lacy leaves and tendrils busy with the unfathomable chemistry of growth and regeneration, minute insects and little feathered and furry things—warm, vibrant, intense life all about us. This we had joined joyously. We had been in fact (from our point of view) the hub of this particular universe.

14

SNOW FELL IN PARADISE VALLEY in October and melted away again. The late flowering gentians were still unfurling their royal blue petals, and the fields of golden arnica and senecio were well peppered with purple asters. These fall flowers, already tardy, could not now pause in their race with the season. They needed a few more days of precious sunshine to mature their seed. Only sharply freezing temperatures would stop them in their fixed design.

But the wild animals, and we not-so-wild humans, took warning from this snow. The striped ground squirrels and the hoary marmots prepared nests for a winter-long hibernation; the rock rabbits and the gray jays who would not hibernate worked feverishly to lay away enormous stores of food. The men who were to be the new winter keepers at the inn followed their example; and we, like the bear and the deer, prepared to migrate downward to milder climates. The white mountain goat had already found lower, safer pastures. Later the bear would hole up for a short period of hibernation in the deeper valleys.

In November heavier snows fell and lay for a week on the ground, but except in the shade of the buildings, these too melted away during a spell of bright, autumn-end sunshine. But now even the sunny days were short, and the little stream by our cabin door was rimmed each morning with spangles and lavalieres of crystal ice. Early-hibernating animals peeped out speculatively on the warmer days, but the late-blooming flowers had either lost the race or won by a frosty hour, and their prostrate stems did not rise again. The great snows were not far away.

It was almost Thanksgiving before winter really settled down in earnest. Even then it did not roar in on icy winds, but like crafty warriors crept quietly in under leaden skies and surrounded us in the night. One morning the trees were bowed down with snow.

By then I had boarded up the office and built a small entrance shelter over the second-story rear door for occasional winter use. Although we would live at Park Headquarters at Longmire Springs, this would be my patrol area.

I called Chief Ranger Barnett to send a truck for our things.

It was still snowing when the truck arrived—huge fluffy flakes that settled slowly on the dead air and piled up like waves of froth over the already burdened trees and bushes. All the lesser detail of the landscape was hidden under this downy blanket, and what was hidden now would remain hidden until late June of the following year. So three strident seasons had been crowded into only five months, and during the long winter season—the remaining seven months of the year—the silent white world of the great mountain would rest. This then was the cycle of the seasons. Already the glaciers were locked in the grip of frost and had all but ceased their grinding.

15

WE DRAGGED THE WOODEN SHUTTERS out from their place beneath the porch and Ruth held them while I nailed them over the doors and windows. This little cabin would quickly disappear beneath the falling snow. We then piled our gear on an old toboggan and with Ken running alongside to steady the load, eased our belongings down the steep hill to where the truck waited beside the road.

The road crews had already placed tall yellow stakes along each side of the highway and by all the guard rails of the bridges, which would guide the steam shovel and the snowplows when they opened the road again in the spring. My duties would bring me back occasionally over the ski trail, but Ruth and Ken would not again see our valley until the chinook winds released it from next spring's snows. By then the sound of rushing water would once more have invaded the silence of winter; avalanche lilies would have pushed waxy buds through the edges of the reluctant snowbanks; bear and marmot would be bringing their little ones to feast newly opened eyes on the bright new world; and, not to be outdone by all of these, Ken would have a brand-new baby sister.

To the old mountain high above, all this I am sure, meant nothing at all. Heat and cold, light and shadow, life and death, time and eternity—of these the mountain was totally unaware. But perhaps the Indians were not wholly wrong when they recognized a spirit dwelling in and over the mountain—a guarding spirit who directed the actions of those who, like ourselves, played brief roles on this vast alpine stage. Who knows—but certainly for three of us life would never be the same again. During all our life the great mountain would be there and never would we look upon it (as we do almost daily from our home on Lake Washington) without knowing that it is one of the benign dynamics of our being.

CPSIA information can be obtained
at www.ICGtesting.com
Printed in the USA
FFHW021421130619
52959034-58563FF

9 780898 866537